SuperVision

SuperVision

AN INTRODUCTION TO
THE SURVEILLANCE SOCIETY

JOHN GILLIOM AND TORIN MONAHAN

The University of Chicago Press   Chicago and London

JOHN GILLIOM is professor in the Department of Political Science at Ohio University. He is the author of *Overseers of the Poor* and *Surveillance, Privacy, and the Law.*

TORIN MONAHAN is associate professor in the Department of Human and Organizational Development at Vanderbilt University. He is the author of several books, including, most recently, *Surveillance in the Time of Insecurity.*

The University of Chicago Press, Chicago 60637
The University of Chicago Press, Ltd., London
© 2013 by The University of Chicago
All rights reserved. Published 2013.
Printed in the United States of America

22 21 20 19 18 17 16 15 14 13   1 2 3 4 5

ISBN-13: 978-0-226-92443-4 (cloth)
ISBN-10: 0-226-92443-2 (cloth)
ISBN-13: 978-0-226-92444-1 (paper)
ISBN-10: 0-226-92444-0 (paper)
ISBN-13: 978-0-226-92445-8 (e-book)
ISBN-10: 0-226-92445-9 (e-book)

Library of Congress Cataloging-in-Publication Data
Gilliom, John, 1960–
    SuperVision: an introduction to the surveillance society / John Gilliom and Torin Monahan.
        pages; cm
    Includes bibliographical references and index.
    ISBN 978-0-226-92443-4 (cloth: alkaline paper) — ISBN 0-226-92443-2 (cloth: alkaline paper) — ISBN 978-0-226-92444-1 (paperback: alkaline paper) — ISBN 0-226-92444-0 (paperback: alkaline paper) — ISBN 978-0-226-92445-8 (e-book) — ISBN 0-226-92445-9 (e-book)   1. Electronic surveillance—Social aspects.
2. Information technology—Social aspects.   3. Privacy, Right of.
I. Monahan, Torin.   II. Title.
    TK7882.E2G55 2012
    363.1′063—dc23   2012014021

♾ This paper meets the requirements of ANSI/NISO Z39.48-1992 (Permanence of Paper).

CONTENTS

PREFACE

Video cameras monitor the streets and sidewalks. Cell phones record locations and messages. Facebook postings share intimate information. Credit card transactions are logged and assessed. A visit to the ATM leaves a data trail. A police officer watches the intersection. A car's on-board computers record location, performance, and driving practices.

A ten-minute errand exposes the typical person to many dimensions of surveillance. Normally they blur into the background of our daily lives—we're usually too busy doing other things to pay attention to these often silent and invisible moments of supervision. This book pushes these moments to the foreground to explore surveillance as an increasingly pervasive element of social life. Our definition of surveillance is broad: we write about everything from your cell phone to drone aircraft, from your Facebook page to antiterrorism initiatives, from your credit card to your Google searches.

In the story we tell, our lives as citizens, students, employees, and consumers are fully embedded in interactive and dynamic webs of surveillance. We'll argue that such vast and transformative changes require a complete reimagining of social life. Our primary goal is to invite readers into this reimagining by providing a crash course in the current practices of surveillance and a set of core questions that can guide the journey. To make this invitation work, we've opted to keep this book short and accessible, with a focus on topics that are relevant to most people's daily lives. We examine mechanisms of surveillance, explore contexts, ask tough questions, and move on; we're trying to give our readers the tools to understand and critically engage, and we don't aspire to have the final word.

As academic researchers, we almost always write for insiders—our colleagues who study surveillance and related issues in society and politics. But as citizens and teachers, we've long felt the need for a book that introduces nonspecialists to the world of surveillance. Here we start in the practical context of everyday life and explore these new phenomena in ways that recognize how little we know and how much we have to learn. Because we aren't writing for insiders, we've avoided many of the formalities that can make academic writing less accessible. You can frolic in the endnotes to see the academic and journalistic works behind what we're covering, but for the most part we keep that stuff backstage to create a more enjoyable read. As a result, this book may frustrate some of our academic colleagues. Some will feel we've oversimplified complicated issues. Others may think we've omitted important locations, tactics, or implications of surveillance. And still others may long for more full-blown explorations of the theoretical and conceptual issues behind our discussions. Our response: This book wasn't written for you. It was written for our students, our friends, our neighbors, and others who might be curious about the world of surveillance.

ACKNOWLEDGMENTS

A book like this is made possible by important contributions from many people. Dozens of our students have helped by reading early chapters, letting us know when it got boring, and supporting our effort to keep it real. Michael Musheno, Kevin Haggerty, and Jill Fisher read drafts of the manuscript and offered valuable critiques and insights. Our colleagues in surveillance studies have taught us a great deal over the years and given us ample material to share. Angelo State University helped launch this collaboration when they invited us to spend three days leading conversations about surveillance during the 2008 E. James Holland Symposium on American Values. John Tryneski, Rodney Powell, and the rest of the team at the University of Chicago Press have offered their strong support in getting the project done and kept up just enough pressure to get it done faster and better. Mary Forfia and Paul Hypolite both went beyond the call of duty in their able research assistance and fact-checking. Finally, we close our acknowledgments with a thank-you to each other—the collaboration that produced this book has been a delight of creativity, exploration, and learning. We can only hope that our readers get as much from it as we have.

Introduction

Are You Under Surveillance?

Let's do a quick check.

Do you have any of these?

- a cell phone
- a credit or debit card
- an identification card

Do you do any of these?

- use Google, Gmail, or Facebook
- go to school
- have a job
- drive a car

If the answer to any of these questions is yes, then you are under surveillance. Every one of these items, places, and activities is a key agent in the overlapping systems of watching, recording, and assessing that make up a "surveillance society."[1] These forms of supervision might take the shape of tracking your cell phone location, calls, and contact information; checking your urine for signs of drug use; or designing a personalized online ad campaign by scanning your e-mail. This book is designed to help you become aware of surveillance, teach you some tricks to deal with it, and provoke new ways of thinking about it.

Our primary audience is those who are vaguely aware that Google keeps track of things but aren't sure what they are. These readers are pretty confident that their cell phones store their locations and calls, but they don't know how it's done, who might use it, or why anyone cares. No one has taught them to use their credit cards in ways that protect their credit ratings or even told them that credit card companies track and analyze purchasing habits. These readers' lives have included standardized tests, school and workplace ID cards, air travel, and online sites like Facebook, but they've never really thought of these things as "surveillance." And they aren't particularly concerned. They've heard people talk about the "right to privacy" and they know journalists carry on about Big Brother, but they really can't see what the big deal is. If any part of this description fits you, then you're in the right place.

The Surveillance Society

Why do we call this a surveillance society? Because virtually all significant social, institutional, or business activities in our society now involve the systematic monitoring, gathering, and analysis of information in order to make decisions, minimize risk, sort populations, and exercise power. We define surveillance as *monitoring people in order to regulate or govern their behavior*. In this book you will see countless ways that surveillance compels new scales and forms of visibility in almost every dimension of our lives. We'll be arguing that the power exercised through these new forms of vision and visibility brings new modes of governance to schools, workplaces, and society at large. This book will not advance one grand theory or argument, because the dimensions and forms of surveillance are too varied, diverse, and shifting to boil it all down to a single take. There are so many types of surveillance, in so many contexts, with so many unimagined developments yet to come that our goal cannot be to reach a definitive conclusion. We hope, rather, to create a broad awareness and raise a set of critical questions.

You've probably heard our times described as the information age or the information society. Information societies are defined by the generation, exchange, and application of data by institutions and individuals; they require communication infrastructures and databases for the functioning of financial markets, industrial production, education, energy systems, voting, communication, transportation, and more. Just try to imagine a major enterprise in your life that doesn't have a developed information management dimension. What's less obvious to most people is that information societies are necessarily surveillance societies. Read that line again: *information societies are necessarily sur-*

veillance societies. That's because organizations and individuals amass data, through electronic and other means, so they can act on it. They make decisions that influence people, that protect or punish people, that divide people into groups and shape their behavior. When information is acted on in these ways, it creates relationships of power and control—it's a form of surveillance.

Confronting Surveillance

This book spends a lot of time exploring new and emergent technologies, but we shouldn't forget that surveillance has been around for a long time. Older, less formal, less technical versions took place as people watched each other within families, small towns, schools, and religious institutions—and they still do. New forms of surveillance emerged as these institutions mutated and became less central in the face of an urbanizing, globalizing, mobile, and growing population. With the dawn of the information age and the wildfire spread of affordable computers, surveillance went high-tech and moved to the center of many dimensions of our lives.

Because of these changes, those of us living in the early decades of the twenty-first century experience a new world. Picture a simple example of the transformation: Wanda B. applies for a mortgage in a small American town sometime in the middle of the twentieth century. She's debt-free and from a well-known family. She's a deaconess at her church, has been in her current job for twenty-five years, and is known for her well-tended home and yard. The white banker turns her down because he's angry that Wanda B. is an African American woman who is a local leader in the civil rights movement. This practice, known as "economic lynching," was used to strip activists of their jobs, homes, insurance, and vehicles.

Fast-forward to 2013: Wanda B.'s granddaughter, Wanda D., is also a politically active African American woman with a tidy home. She doesn't attend church, but she has a steady job and her credit score is a stellar 822. The credit score is derived from surveillance of her credit card use, her bill-paying habits, her debt-to-income ratio, and other criteria. It does not factor in race, church attendance, or political activism. The banker has never met Wanda D., but she approves her loan application based on a couple of forms and the magic 822.

This example illustrates the rising importance of institutional surveillance, data-driven decision making, and the powerful mathematics of the credit-reporting industry. But it also shows that the seemingly heartless and technocratic surveillance that shapes our times has *the potential* to be a wonderful and liberating thing. It can make it more difficult for personal power and racism to affect important decisions. Modern surveillance can also make it easier to catch dangerous criminals. It can help first responders find locations and rescue people. It can help teachers identify struggling students and help colleges, graduate programs, and employers identify qualified applicants. Contemporary surveillance programs also make sure that the advertising on your Internet browser reflects your interests, that your software updates are punctual, and that you get helpful recommendations from online businesses like Amazon.com, Gmail, Netflix, and iTunes. In all these ways, surveillance is critical in helping people, businesses, and governments do their jobs.

But plenty of other examples give a different view of surveillance. Even though Wanda D. got her loan, the credit-scoring industry can make things extra hard for most low-income and minority citizens. Because lower credit scores plague lower-income groups, which, as you no doubt know, have higher proportions of African Americans and Latinos, credit scores work as one more tool in the system that cements historical inequalities. That's because lower credit scores not only make it more difficult to get a loan; they make the loan more expensive by driving up fees and interest rates.[2] And, as you'll see later in this book, a low credit score can also make car insurance more expensive and even make it tougher to find a job or a place to live.

Along with the many stories we'll see about the clever things modern surveillance can do for us, there are stories about more troubling applications. Here are some quick examples. After the 2009 pro-democracy demonstrations in Iran, the Iranian government and cell phone giant Nokia cooperated to use cell phone records to track down and jail the movement's leaders. From 2009 to 2010, school officials in Lower Merion, Pennsylvania, tapped into the remote-control camera function on school laptops to snap photographs of kids in their bedrooms. An insurance company used Facebook photos of a woman smiling to deny her disability claim for depression. And security guards and police have been known to employ video surveillance to profile people of color and to spy on young women. Some of these stories are scary, others just a bit creepy, but they're reminders that there's more to surveillance than easy credit, rescued hikers, and well-targeted ads.

Each day, with each new technology, we grow more accustomed to the surveillance society. This will be one of our central themes. Whether we're gaming, shopping, texting, or watching TV, we're generating data for others to scrutinize in the online world. If we're driving, our cell phone, GPS, iPad, or OnStar system constantly monitors our location, while the "black boxes" in newer cars record driving behavior. At work, school, and the doctor's office, digital portfolios burst with data about our assessed characteristics, talents, and conditions. And most of us tend to like and appreciate it. Perhaps not all of these surveillance measures are of great importance on their own. But taken together, they describe important, large-scale changes in the way people and institutions operate. By the end of this book, you should have a pretty good idea of what these changes look like and mean.

The Three Big Denials

When asked your opinion of surveillance, you might say something like "I've got nothing to hide." In our experience as teachers and speakers, many people are interested in exploring the implications and politics of the surveillance society, but there's always a subset looking to shrug it off and avoid the conversation. Here's a special section for those folks.

If you get by thinking that "no one cares about little ol' me," we urge you to think again. You may live a fairly obscure life, but you're a valuable commodity to some, a security risk to others, a future customer or potential voter to still more. This isn't to say there aren't different degrees of exposure. If you're young, pay with cash, avoid a cell phone, stay off Facebook, and keep away from the health, banking, and online retail industries as well as the military and law-enforcement systems, you're going to have less of a profile. But most of us either can't or won't avoid all these types of engagement and therefore would be better off understanding how the surveillance society works.

If you *are* one of the many people who say something like "If you don't do anything wrong, you don't have anything to worry about," we think you'll have a different view when you finish this book. In the surveillance society, definitions of "wrong" shift and vary and can include things like participating in political demonstrations, having poor health, losing your job, being young, getting old, being male, being female, or belonging to any racial or ethnic group on the planet. In short, there are so many different and conflicting definitions of *wrong* that we're all doing something wrong all the time. That's in large part because institutions are looking for different types of wrong. It's not just classics like smoking dope or shoplifting—techniques of surveillance are on the watch for any person or pattern that can present a risk. So, in the end, since each of us presents some sort of risk to some institution at some point in our lives, we're all doing something wrong. But the rise of the surveillance society also means that those things you do "right" should also worry or, better, *concern* you in the sense that you need to attend to them and be aware of your digital persona. Credit ratings need to be monitored and managed for signs of fraud or error. The same thing goes for school, health, and insurance records, in addition to the many other registries that document our lives. In these ways, we're taught to engage in a kind of self-surveillance in order to manage our data images.

Finally, if you believe that your privacy is being protected by laws and user agreements, think again. In Western Europe, you may have slightly better protection through government privacy regulations, but by and large the famous "right to privacy" is not well enforced. There are many books you can read about the ups and downs of privacy.[3] Our perspective is that in the face of rapidly advancing technology— coupled with nearly unchecked power for law enforcement, the military, and corporations all wanting to implement new technologies—the promise that the right to privacy may have once offered is being quickly outstripped.

Okay, so we've introduced you to a complex and threatening reality *and* knocked down the most popular denials and coping mechanisms. Sorry about that. But we want to be clear that you've *got* to know about this stuff. So where do we go from here?

Rethinking Surveillance

It would be easy for us to write a short, shallow book called *Big Brother and the Death of Privacy!* or *Surveillance to the Rescue! Safety, Shopping, and Savings in the New Information Economy*. We could probably sell thousands of copies and maybe even get on a few talk shows. But these simple, well-worn takes on a complicated subject don't do justice to the intriguing contradictions of living in a surveillance society. We've been able to stay interested in surveillance for many years because there are so many things to learn and think about. It never gets old because we find ourselves in a rapidly changing world that constantly invites us to ask—and try to answer—challenging new questions.

In the struggle to ask and answer new questions, we need to abandon some of the old frameworks. For example, we believe that terms like *Big Brother* and *privacy* are out-of-date and no longer help describe the dynamic new forms of technology, power, and politics. We also believe that simplistic dichotomies mislead us: surveillance versus privacy and freedom versus security are superficial ways to structure an argument. They might make for a dramatic little debate, but they don't do much to help us think creatively about deep new issues.

The result of these obsolete terms and conventional wisdoms is that people have gotten kind of dumb when it comes to surveillance. We can watch a couple of on-air personalities have a fiery debate about privacy, security, and Big Brother and convince ourselves we've done a good job at being informed citizens. We haven't. There's *a lot* more going on here, and that's what we hope to show you. And by the way, we're not going to just invent some new words as if we have all the answers. Since we don't yet know what the "right" new vocabulary is, this book focuses on exploring this new world *and* the ideas and terms that can help us better understand it.

What's the Big Idea?

(Actually, there are several.)

Before we dive into the main part of the book, we want to briefly introduce what we consider the most important arguments or ideas. We've already hinted at some of them, but since this isn't a mystery novel, we're going to be as straightforward as possible.

The Ten Big Ideas

1. The established vocabulary and entrenched ideas like privacy and Big Brother can't do justice to our new and complex situation. These influential concepts can contribute to our dialogue, but their reign in the world of surveillance has got to end. A smarter way to think about today's surveillance begins with a fresh reckoning of the nature and

implications of a rapidly changing array of technologies and policies. It means looking at how surveillance is really used, who's using it, and how it affects our world. It means understanding surveillance as a form of power and governance woven into the fabric of our lives. Surveillance is no longer a brief intrusion or a scary idea from a movie, it's a way of life. It's *our* way of life.

2. Surveillance doesn't always come out of the dark recesses of Big Brother's evil scheming—at first glance, some types of surveillance look like fun and don't seem to threaten values like liberty, equality, or democratic governance. Most previous books about surveillance place almost complete emphasis on the negatives. There's nothing wrong with that because skepticism is an essential part of critical thinking. But there's also some enjoyable, engaging, and productive stuff going on, and we're going to explore it.

3. Picturing "big government" as the principal source of modern surveillance is wrong. Governments are important players, but most of the innovative new surveillance initiatives are coming from the corporate sector, which frequently links up with governments in a contractual relationship. We'll argue for reimagining the classic public/private divide so we can better grasp the contemporary fusion of corporate and government power.

4. Surveillance does more than just watch. Surveillance programs definitely "watch" us, although an actual visual dimension is often missing. But in watching the world, surveillance also *shapes* our "selves" by creating odd edited versions of who we are (a test score, a driving record, a credit risk) to form the basis for decisions about us. And surveillance also *makes* our world by establishing patterns of reward and punishment that guide our choices and behaviors. Goals, ideals, taboos, sanctions, rewards—*values*—are part of any surveillance program. As we orient our behavior around the values expressed through surveillance, our lives and our worlds take on new forms.

5. It is incomplete to think of surveillance *only* as something forced on an unwilling populace. It certainly is that in many places and times, but we also have to acknowledge the surveillance programs that people sign up for, support, or even do to themselves. No one ordered us to get cell phones, but when we did, we logged ourselves in to one of the best surveillance networks ever devised. No one makes us post compromising photographs or other content on social networking sites, but for

some reason we do. Our tendency to desire some types of surveillance is a fascinating dimension of the surveillance society.

6. Surveillance challenges the ways we typically think about space and time. Your credit card company can be "watching" you from halfway around the world. Your blog posting today will be a retrievable part of your life far into the future. A grade in a college course is forever. Even a simple life involves a complicated juggling of different social worlds, contexts, and people—it gets immensely more complicated when the normal boundaries of space and time erode to open each moment to the possibility of global permanence.

7. There may be a massive uncelebrated anti-surveillance movement formed by all the people who cheat, lie, evade, trick, or otherwise undermine surveillance programs. These activities, sometimes called "everyday resistance," are a controversial part of the politics of surveillance because they often fall into a gray area that is not quite crime, not quite politics, not quite honorable, but sometimes noble. In a world of ubiquitous monitoring, everyday resistance is a frequent and perhaps necessary element.

8. Systems of surveillance are often unique new expressions of power, but they join existing social patterns tied to inequalities of race, class, and gender. Sometimes new programs challenge these patterns. Other times they advance them. While something like financial surveillance may become more color-blind, surveillance at border crossings brings seemingly inevitable intensifications of race-oriented profiling.

9. As pervasive and impressive as surveillance systems are, they don't always work. Or, more accurately, they don't always produce the desired or promised results. Security cameras don't really prevent crime, though they can sometimes move it elsewhere or help police identify and apprehend suspects. Amazon.com shopping recommendations can be comically wrong. And a student's performance on a standardized test may be a horrible predictor of academic ability or success. Surveillance may not work perfectly, but people still believe in it and act on it.

10. Scientific rationalism is the dominant mentality of our time, leading to an insatiable hunger for information. Because of this, organizations are almost always pro-surveillance. Governments, corporations, courts, and individuals all seek information so they can make smart choices. This is in many ways the modern definition of responsible de-

cision making. In this world, is there any room for anti-surveillance claims that argue for, essentially, reducing the flow of information?

Since we've organized this book around the nature and impact of surveillance in everyday life, the chapters do not strictly follow the agenda expressed by the Ten Big Ideas. You'll find the big ideas in the background discussions and occasional text boxes. You should also be able to detect them in the way we present and analyze examples. But we're not going to obsess: our aim is to generate thought, not give lectures.

Plan of the Book

This little book is going to deliver a lot of information about the surveillance society and push for original critical thinking about the social and political implications of our new world. We use everyday items, activities, or places to trace and explore surveillance in context. Thus, cell phones (chapter 1), credit and identification cards (chapter 2), and the Internet (chapter 3) plug most people into the matrix of the surveillance society. Organizations like schools (chapter 4) or workplaces (chapter 5) embed people in a whole host of surveillance relationships and dependencies that are largely unavoidable. And security systems (chapter 6), whether at airports or on city streets, epitomize contemporary surveillance and make grand promises of safety and security that they may never achieve. The conclusion picks up the conversation started here and presents our closing thoughts. Finally, at the end there's a list of recommended readings and resources that shows where you can go for more work on the themes and issues raised in each chapter.[4]

1: My Cell, My Self

The cell phone has eclipsed the Swiss Army knife as the perfect all-in-one tool and toy. From music to money management to e-mail, texting, shopping, research, games, photos, movies, directions, calendars, and even phone calls, this little gadget does it all. In a pinch, it even works as a flashlight. Yours is probably within reach right now. And by the time this book is in print, the list of things you can do with a cell phone will be even longer.

Cell phones are also the perfect symbol of the surveillance society. With the right technology or a little help from a service provider, your cell phone lets the curious know who you are, who your friends are, where you are, and where you've been. With cell phone information, authorities have been able to find lost hikers, rescue kidnapped children, convict mob hit men, and jail political activists. But cell phones aren't all about tracking and finding. Add a bit of extra software and cell phones become roving bugs, allowing remote users to listen in on any conversation in the phones' vicinity. As we'll see, they also mobilize an army of 300 million photographers able to take and transmit still and video images of everything from police misconduct to dorm parties.

To begin rethinking your cell phone from a surveillance perspective, just imagine this (totally fake) news report:

Washington. In legislation signed by the president, the United States government mandated that all citizens carry an electronic device providing live-streamed data on their location, communication activity, and personal interactions. Data banks will constantly record the time, duration, sender, and receiver of all telephone calls and electronic transmissions, while targeted investigations will be able to monitor actual conversations and message content. Cross-analysis of multiparty location records will show patterns of personal interaction and association.

The new program also creates what one official called "300 million eyes" by requiring that each of the mandated devices be equipped with an advanced digital camera able to record and document evidence and transmit it to authorities.

Officials from police, national security, and public health and safety agencies heralded the move. In the words of one, "This brings an end to the darkness. We can now better serve our citizens with a universal capacity to know where everyone is, all the time. We'll know who they're with, who they talk to, when they move, and where they go. This is a massive improvement in our ability to control disease, crime, and terrorism."

To offset the cost of the program, each citizen will be required to pay a monthly fee.

This news story may be fake, but the outcome is real. Except for the government mandate, this is exactly what the cell phone revolution has achieved—monthly fee and all!

There are roughly 300 million cell phone subscribers in the United States and its territories, while the worldwide figure is ready to top 5.3 billion.[1] That's a phenomenal rate of growth when you realize that pocket-size phones weren't even available until the early 1990s. And it's a startling level of saturation, with roughly 90 percent of Americans now using cell phones.[2] But how many of these people understand the basics of how their phone works or what it can do for them (or *to* them)?

How Things Work

The next couple of pages provide a quick technical overview of how cell phones work and how they fit into the surveillance society. We'll show that the communication and billing functions of our phones make them handy tracking devices. Furthermore, newer features and applications like built-in global positioning systems (GPS), Bluetooth capabilities, and mapping software add more sophisticated means of tapping, tracing, and locating. Finally, we'll turn to one of the most popular features, the camera, and discuss its unique and fascinating place in the surveillance tool kit.

The first thing to point out is that if you have or are part of a service plan, your cell phone knows who you are and shares your identity with the world. Phones contain unique identifying numbers that are transmitted whenever the phone is on. Since these numbers correspond to an account and thus a person, anonymity is difficult to achieve in the cellular world. Some prepaid "go phones" that don't require you to sign up for a plan may seem to provide anonymity, but even they can be used to track and identify the user, since the numbers one calls and the places one goes reveal the user's social network, daily activities, and eventually identity. Anyone closely monitoring and analyzing the data could probably figure it out.

But your phone tells the world a lot more than simply who you are. Other characteristics are logged in routine data collection, and some are right on your bill. This includes whom you call or text, as well as the time, duration, and frequency of your contacts. We can also learn how often you roam to other regions or area codes, how often you leave the country, and which countries you visit. Other information is generated by how you use your phone, even if the data don't appear on your bill. For instance, a lot can be learned about your interests and social networks by watching how you use Twitter, Flickr, Facebook, or other applications to send messages or pictures to the Internet: what you upload, where you upload it, who responds to you, what images you tag, whom you're tagged with in uploaded images, and so on. A detailed, if partial and skewed, portrait of you can be gleaned from this information. But there's more to it.

So your phone marks who you are and who's in your circle, but how does it tell where you are? There are at least four ways your location can be tracked: through cell towers, GPS, WiFi, and Bluetooth. A cell phone is basically a fancy three-channel radio—one channel talks, one channel listens, a third channel arranges communication with the system. Let's talk about that third, quiet channel. When a cell phone is on, it's in steady communication with the now ubiquitous cell towers and antennae—known as sites. That's because the equipment needs to figure out which sites will handle the signal from your regularly moving phone. Even if a call or data transfer is not being made, the service provider's equipment actively monitors the identity, direction, and strength of the signal. Because the towers monitor the identification and signal direction of each cell phone, and because multiple towers allow "triangulation" on a particular phone, its location can always be tracked. Through this particular process, your location can be narrowed to within a couple of hundred yards in urban areas that have multiple antennae.[3]

Cell Phone Protests

An international boycott commenced after it was learned that the Nokia Corporation, the world's largest cell phone manufacturer and a major provider of cell phones in Iran, sold the Iranian government a surveillance and control center that enabled it to track and limit communications during a wave of pro-democracy rallies in 2009.[4] The boycott expressed widespread popular anger over Nokia's complicity in the Iranian government's efforts to monitor phone traffic, scramble and jam service, and listen in on conversations. According to the boycott organizers, hundreds were jailed "thanks to Nokia's technology."[5] Just as cell phones and social media were influential tools used by protestors in Iran and, later on, in other countries during the 2011 revolutionary movement known as the Arab Spring, these technologies also open people up to extraordinarily repressive forms of social control.

But triangulation is old news. Unless you've had your phone for years, it also includes a legally mandated GPS, which can disclose your location with pinpoint accuracy—typically within fifty feet. Phones registered in the United States and Canada are now linked in with the E911 service. This service is intended to coordinate emergency responses by, for instance, automatically marking your location when you dial 911. With this, of course, comes the capacity for constant surveillance of your travels.[6] Many advanced cell phones are *always* signaling their location, even when they're turned off. The implications of these new capabilities require no speculation: for a modest fee, police authorities have convenient access to Sprint web portals, for instance, which allowed them to undertake *8 million* cell phone GPS location checks in 2009 alone.[7] And that's just one company.

Ordinary citizens can approximate this kind of tracking through mobile phone applications such as Google Latitude, which encourages people to extend their social networking activities into physical space.[8] Latitude users can track the precise location of willing friends, family members, or others and watch them move across a map. According to a Google spokesperson, "This adds a social flavor to Google maps and makes it more fun."[9] This fun, much like Twitter and other interactive applications for sharing information, introduces the potential for generating massive amounts of personal data, although Google claims to be uninterested in stockpiling or selling e-data to marketers—at least for the moment.[10]

Most smartphones (like iPhones, Androids, or Blackberries) are also WiFi devices that continuously scout for available networks so that data can be pushed to the device, even if you're not actively surfing the web or checking e-mail. WiFi networks, as you may already know, are assigned unique IP (Internet protocol) addresses that are tied to physical locations—like someone's home address or the pizza place on the corner. When your phone uses these networks, it promiscuously reveals the IP address, essentially saying to the world, "I'm here! In this city, on this street, in this building!" That may increase the functionality of your apps so that you can get accurate directions or recommendations to nearby restaurants, but it also means that your location is always known.

What's more, your phone is archiving *all* your locations and movements, creating a highly detailed story of your mobile life, just waiting for the FBI, or hackers, or your creepy stalker ex-boyfriend to access and exploit. Apple iPhones store all location data in a file on the phones and routinely beam them up to the Apple mother ship, but anyone accessing your phone (physically or remotely) could also learn all your previous locations.[11] And Google's Android phones promote unwelcome uses of this sort by making the previous locations of your phone publicly available on the Internet for anyone to see. All someone has to do is capture your device's unique hardware number (also known as a Media Access Control [MAC] address), which WiFi networks do automatically, and courtesy of Google they could discover your previous locations, such as your home address, the coffee shop you visit every Thursday afternoon at 2:15, the works.[12] The potential for abuse is high.

There are also new surveillance functions opened up by Bluetooth-enabled phones, headsets, or other devices that share your information within a smaller radius (about thirty feet). For example, shopping malls can set up Bluetooth surveillance networks to track where people shop and for how long or to send specific messages related to the shopper's location. This was just what the Aalborg Zoo in Denmark did to find out which animals and attractions visitors found most popular; they even offered "bluetags" to help parents track their children.[13] (Be careful with your Bluetooth: "bluesnarfing" hackers can access a Bluetoother's address book, e-mail, and call history or even hijack a phone remotely to make calls and send messages.[14])

Moreover, there are reported cases of FBI agents surreptitiously re-programming cell phone software to convert cell phones into remote microphones—"roving bugs"—to listen to face-to-face conversations occurring near the phone, even when the phone is turned off.[15] This is how incriminating evidence was collected on mobsters in the Genovese crime family in New York, leading to arrests in 2006 for labor racke-teering and other charges. Various online businesses, such as FlexiSPY, purport to make this sort of eavesdropping available to anyone who can pay $350 a year and get her hands on the target phone for fifteen min-utes.[16] Soon, we expect, you won't even need that fifteen minutes with the phone, since software will allow remote enabling. If this surprises you, think about some of the games, songs, and apps you've downloaded—it's not much harder to remotely insert a small software application to enhance the surveillance functions just as you'd download a game.[17]

It's the Latest: "Augmented Reality"

A new software protocol known as augmented reality allows phone users to hold their phone cameras up to "tagged" objects in the world (movie post-ers, restaurants, artwork, etc.) to receive additional information about them. With some augmented reality applications, users can affix their own virtual tags to objects or places so others can find and view them; this practice has the potential to exponentially increase the number of things tagged in this material-virtual hybrid space. When people voluntarily tag items, though, they are also leaving behind a remainder: a digital fingerprint that links them to those spaces at certain times.

Between billing records, triangulation, GPS, WiFi, Bluetooth, and tracking applications, the little device in your pocket or bag makes you constantly knowable and mappable. This can be a great thing, since you may find yourself lost in a national forest, trapped in a remote area with a car breakdown, or, perhaps worse, downtown on a Saturday night with no friends in sight. Once you alert someone, not only will help be on the way; it should be able to find the right place.[18]

In an interesting twist, cell phones also turn the user into a rov-ing surveillance unit, because most phones now have a built-in camera that allows you to shoot and transmit videos and stills of anything you see. When the National Association for the Advancement of Colored People (NAACP) celebrated its hundredth anniversary, it launched a website that allows people to upload footage of police misconduct for its legal team to review.[19] Others have used cell phone cameras to take voyeuristic photos in locker rooms or public settings, and some turn to online posting sites specializing in such material. You've also, no doubt, uploaded and viewed plenty of cell phone shots on social networking sites.

This dimension of the cell phone's surveillance capacity can challenge the way we usually think about surveillance—as something done by large powers like governments and corporations. And though we're not entirely sure that one individual snapping a quick picture counts as "surveillance," it seems clear that the sum total of all those quick pics adds an important new dimension to the surveillance society. To put it bluntly, we've shifted to a new level of ongoing scrutiny when we live in a society with over 300 million cameras waiting to record and broadcast anything we do. We're observed today in many ways that most of us probably take for granted and don't even see as surveillance.

The Volunteer Army

No one ordered you to get a cell phone. As one of the most rapidly spreading personal technologies in history, cell phones have permeated the population in a stunningly short time. As status symbol, mobility enhancer, safety tool, toy, camera, web browser, address book, and more, it's hard to beat these multifaceted devices. When a surveillance technology is gladly, even fervently, adopted by a population, things get interesting. If you think about some of the iconic images of surveillance—prisons, IRS audits, final exams— you don't picture joyous throngs clamoring to wrap their arms around them. But the beauty of cell phones—and we'll see this with things like credit cards and social networking sites as well—is that we sign up and we like it, or at least most of us do. (And in case you're wondering, yes, the authors also have and enjoy cell phones, credit cards, iToys, and many of the other must-have accessories of the surveillance society. We're all in this together.)

Expanding Surveillance

Cell phones enable extensive surveillance of your location, your electronic communication, your social interaction, your conversations, and the events happening around you. But chances are, until you started reading this book, you didn't think of your cell phone as a surveillance device. That's because the word *surveillance* is too often tied to things like video cameras, government spying programs, and black vans full of geeks wearing large headphones—potent symbols that simply don't represent the full range of surveillance in society. One of our main goals is to expand your understanding of surveillance by demonstrating how it works in daily life. But before we show you more, we've got to spend a little time developing a broader and richer conceptualization of the very idea of surveillance. In the pages that follow, we argue that fundamental changes in the breadth and nature of surveillance compel a wider and more nuanced understanding of the term. We then move on to a broader questioning of some of the other famous terms in the surveillance vocabulary, like *Big Brother*, the *panopticon*, and the *right to privacy*.

In the introduction, we wrote that surveillance could be thought of as *monitoring people in order to regulate or govern their behavior*. Surveillance, in other words, is an exercise of power through watching. In the social sciences, "power" has been classically (and too simply) defined as the ability to get people to do something they would not otherwise do. We've all had the experience of changing our behavior when we realize someone is watching us; if observation can make people do (or not do) something, then it can be understood as a form of power. When we note that the term *surveillance* comes from the French word meaning "to watch from above," the emphasis on "above" implies that power relationship.

Surveillance is not new, and it certainly doesn't require a lot of digital equipment. Increasingly, though, age-old techniques of watching and listening are being complemented and enhanced by technological means. Today's digital technologies emit a steady stream of information about us: whom we call or text, where we are, where we shop, what we buy, how fast we drive, what websites we visit, who our "friends" are, what music we listen to, what TV shows we watch, how productive we are at work, how well we do in school, the likelihood of our getting sick or wrecking our cars, and so on. The many electronic devices we use create vast quantities of data about us, allowing others to scrutinize our activities, preferences, accomplishments, and failures.

In the "good old days," surveillance typically meant being physically watched by someone visible and familiar—like a parent or a boss. But now, because our data both live long and travel well, we're often watched by others who aren't physically present, who are unknown to us, who may be studying us at a later time, and whose motives are diverse, changing, or unclear. These new realities call for a revised understanding of "surveillance" that places less emphasis on a relationship between two people at one time and place. Data drawn from your cell phone and other devices can be used by many different people for different goals at different times. "Your" data may not even be used to study you! They might be used to piece together information about others or to study and manage the behavior of large clusters of individuals. So when talking about surveillance and power, we need to realize it's not just about someone getting us to do things we don't want to do. Instead, institutions, architecture, and technologies mobilize power so that we're enmeshed in surveillant relationships just by moving through the world, even without an explicit gaze from above.[20] Sometimes we desire those relationships, and lots of times we're probably not even aware of them.

What Will This Look Like Fifteen Years from Now?

As surveillance is detached from a specific context and moment, codes for appropriate conduct become ambiguous, requiring a lot more foresight, intuition, and caution as we attempt to negotiate our world. If we can't hear the stern reprimand or see the smile or scowl, how can we correct the way we're acting? If we have to be thinking about a scowl (or loss of employment or insurance coverage) that might happen in fifteen years, how do we even begin to manage our lives? Because of these changes, we need to rethink our current understanding of the seemingly natural limits of time and space. For instance, if you're a college or high school student, a Facebook posting about a party you went to over the weekend is probably an appropriate piece of information for your current social context and group of friends. But that same information could be incriminating if a prospective employer views it five or ten years from now.[21] Because of the temporal and spatial ambiguity introduced by digital media, we may feel the effects of surveillance for years to come. Young people thus are being admonished—even by the president of the United States—to be careful what they put on social networking websites.[22]

Please Check Your Baggage at the Curb: Rethinking Our Surveillance Vocabulary

People have been thinking and talking about surveillance for a long time. Because of this, we've accumulated a lot of intellectual baggage in the ways we conceptualize or imagine this necessarily abstract idea. That's one of the key reasons this book focuses on very real things like your cell phone—we want to move away from the sweeping generalities that too often drive our thinking. There will certainly be some big thinking going on, but we want to make sure it's grounded in practical and tangible parts of our everyday lives. So, before we get too far into the book, let's take a quick look at some of the leading images and metaphors in the literature about surveillance, then think about the ways something like cell phone surveillance does or doesn't fit with them. We've already talked about one key term: *surveillance* itself. You might have come to this book with specific images of helicopters and police vans, but we're urging you to picture it as a much broader class of practices including many types of observation, communication, monitoring, and assessment. Some of the other grand terms in the ongoing story of surveillance include *Big Brother*, the *panopticon*, and the beleaguered, embattled, and much-admired *right to privacy.*

Big Brother, from George Orwell's novel *Nineteen Eighty-Four*, is probably the most famous bogeyman and symbol of a surveillance society. In Orwell's dystopic Oceania, citizens are closely watched for signs of ideological or personal deviation from the norm. Reactions to deviance are terrifying in their cruelty and violence. Civil society (private groups like churches, clubs, and businesses) do not exist, and families have been co-opted by the totalitarian state. In a famous quotation, Orwell describes life with Big Brother:

It was terribly dangerous to let your thoughts wander when you were in any public place or within range of a telescreen. The smallest thing could give you away. A nervous tic, an unconscious look of anxiety, a habit of muttering to yourself—anything that carried with it the suggestion of abnormality, of having something to hide. In any case, to wear an improper expression on your face . . . was itself a punishable offense. There was even a word for it in Newspeak: *facecrime*, it was called.[23]

But obviously this imagery doesn't really make sense of *our* world. For most of us, the government is not a despotic totalitarian force watching our every move for the slightest sign of deviation. For most of us, surveillance comes not from a unitary state bent only on domination and control, but from a chaotic blend of government, media, work, friends, family, insurance companies, bankers, and automated

FIGURE 1.1. Modern panopticon: Stateville Correctional Center, Joliet, Illinois, USA. Photograph from Doug Dubois and Jim Goldberg/Magnum Photos.

data-processing systems. Much of the surveillance in our lives is non-threatening—hardly the sense we get from Orwell's classic dystopia.

The same sort of problems surrounds another leading image of surveillance—the *panopticon*. (*Pan* means "all," and *optic* means "seeing.") The panopticon was a prison conceived in the 1700s and made famous in the twentieth-century work of the late French intellectual Michel Foucault.[24] The panopticon is a cylindrical building surrounding a central guard tower, with individual cells built into its outer walls (see fig. 1.1). Cells are backlit and completely observable so that the guards in the central tower could easily watch the inmates. Blinds on the tower windows prevented prisoners from viewing guards, meaning they could never really know when they were being watched. The idea of the panopticon was to use constant observation and a gentle system of regimented discipline to train inmates away from even the possibility of disobedience. They would, in Foucault's words, become "docile bodies" so accustomed to constant observation that they internalized discipline and lost the capacity to resist. Foucault traced the idea of the panopticon out into other sites—like hospitals, schools, and factories—to argue that panopticism had emerged as a defining mode of power in our time.

Now, obviously we think that surveillance and observation *are* defining modes of power in our time. That's one of the key points of this book. Foucault's writings about power helped galvanize a fundamental rethinking of the politics of surveillance as late twentieth-century scholars struggled to confront new forms of systematic observation and control. But, as with Orwell's Big Brother, there are important differences between our reality and the image of the panopticon. We are watched not from a single site, but by many actors in many contexts with many motives, and we're not always aware that we might be seen. And whereas Foucault thought that reproducing the panopticon model throughout societies would subject everyone to a uniform disciplining gaze, surveillance systems today are geared more toward finding or creating *differences* among people and sorting them into finely differentiated categories (according to risk, value, preference, class, status, age, sex, race, and so on).[25] So we're quite unlike the prisoners in the panopticon.

This recognition has led surveillance analysts to sketch out the idea of the *surveillant assemblage*—a concept that shifts our attention away from a central actor or place like Big Brother or the panopticon to focus on the shifting, changing construction of surveillance that threads through the many dimensions of our lives. The surveillant assemblage removes individuals and practices from social context, translating them into "data" that can be analyzed in discrete form, exchanged freely, and recombined to provide a seemingly objective representation—or "data double"—of individuals.[26] The assemblage includes many of the things covered in this book: the watching by teachers, bosses, insurance companies, police officers, Gmail, iTunes, Netflix, Facebook, telecommunications companies, the SAT, the FBI, the credit industry, and all the other players in the surveillance society. The central idea is that *there is no central force: no Big Brother, no panopticon, but a shifting, moving observation, presentation, and regulation of the self by countless measures in countless locations.*

Your cell phone is a great example of this. At a surveillance extreme, your location, calls dialed and received, call contents, text messages, music, videos, photos, and all other transactions can be monitored or tracked by a shifting array of friends, family, service providers, private detectives, the police, or random strangers who find your phone. Much disclosure is voluntary (such as letting friends know where you are), some is coerced (such as iPhone games or marketing schemes that require you to disclose your location), and some is obligatory (such as FBI-mandated GPS location tracking). But these data trails are quickly crossing each other and doubling back, becoming muddy and confused, making distinctions among voluntary, coerced, and obligatory more difficult to perceive. The uses or implications of all one's cell phone data remain unclear and may become important only in hindsight.

Beyond Privacy

You might be surprised to find that you're not going to read much here about the idea of privacy—what one Supreme Court justice famously called the "right to be let alone."[27] This omission is pretty close to a "thoughtcrime" in some circles, and it may seem strange that a book about surveillance doesn't say a whole lot about privacy. After all, privacy is what surveillance invades, right?

Well, sure. Yet now that surveillance is not just an isolated practice but a comprehensive mode of social organization, the implications and issues go way beyond the relatively simple and limited idea of privacy. In the coming chapters, we'll see that practices of surveillance are complicit in things like

- extending and changing the nature and reach of government and corporate power;
- altering the ways we think about time and space;
- creating new templates for individual identity;
- setting new ethics and standards for human behavior;
- enforcing existing inequalities and patterns of social discrimination.

That's important stuff that goes far beyond a mere intrusion on your privacy.

The reason we don't say much about privacy is not that we don't like it or support it. Both of us enjoy our privacy (one is even a little nutso about it). We also think privacy is an important part of the conversation about surveillance. Across the world, attorneys, activists, intellectuals, and civil society groups use privacy arguments (and other claims) in an ongoing effort to limit or regulate surveillance intrusions.[28] But privacy has spent so much time as the top big idea in discussions about surveillance that it has suppressed other ways of thinking. So in this book we ask you to do the same thing with privacy as we've asked you to do with Big Brother and the panopticon: treat it skeptically. These various concepts may be useful intellectual tools, but they're also intellectual baggage inherited from different times and places. They have their uses, but they may also be very limited and limiting.

Try This at Home!
Talk about the implications of cell phone surveillance, but don't let anyone use the word *privacy*. How does eliminating the P-word push the conversation into new areas?

Social Architecture

For us, one of the most productive ways to rethink the powers of surveillance is to think about surveillance technologies as social architecture. Like all technologies, surveillance systems create pathways and opportunities for human and institutional behavior. We typically think of human beings as having relatively unfettered "agency" or choice. But this agency is heavily constrained or shaped by physical and technological limits and properties.[29]

A simple example might be a staircase in a school building. Sure, we *could* get to the second floor by climbing a ladder up the outer wall, but we won't because there's a staircase designed and built to ease our way. We're going to use it, and we'd get in trouble if we didn't. So the staircase shapes human practice by creating opportunities, which are then coupled with expectations. Other examples might be walls that keep people out, sidewalks that guide our paths, busy roads that pedestrians can't easily cross, or classroom layouts where students sit in neat rows visible to the centrally located teacher. Technological constraints can also take the form of digital systems, such as cell phones that keep you accessible and track your travels; key cards that open doors and record your passage; media players that use digital rights management (DRM) software to prevent you from sharing songs; or free e-mail accounts, such as Gmail, that provide no-cost service but automatically review your e-mails and share the content with Google and its partners.

Technologies create pathways for behavior. That's one of the main reasons they're so useful. One way this is important for a discussion of surveillance is in helping us think about how much new technologies should concern us. Right now, you might look around at corporations and governments and conclude that new surveillance technologies don't worry you because you never misbehave, you generally trust your government, you qualify for free shipping, and you're getting all the downloads you could ever want. Other readers might be wary either because they do misbehave or because they're from a population that's been victimized by surveillance.

But if we accept the argument that technologies shape human behavior and adaptations, the rise of the surveillance society should be a critical concern to everyone. Think about it. We now have the ability to track, monitor, assess, and locate virtually every citizen on most meaningful dimensions of their lives. There are so many law enforcement, national security, consumer convenience, public health, profitability, and public safety arguments for making full use of that information that it's really only a matter of time before it's fully harnessed. And with that harnessing, of course, the nature of our society is changing. A larger, more powerful, more intimate, more knowing state and corporate apparatus is the virtually unavoidable outcome of our new technological capacities. That staircase to the second floor has been built—people are going to use it.

Conclusion

Your cell phone is a powerful and complicated piece of communication and surveillance equipment that exposes you to a host of different types of tracking, monitoring, analysis, and inspection. If George Orwell could have imagined it, he would have put it in *Nineteen Eighty-Four*; if Michel Foucault were alive, he'd probably write about it; and privacy advocates around the world are profoundly concerned about the unleashing of this new power. But we've argued that since concepts like Big Brother, the panopticon, and privacy aren't a good fit with our current world, they're not well suited to helping us make sense of it. We support a messier way of thinking.

Because organizations and individuals today thrive on the production and management of information, much of which is digital, search-able, and remotely accessible, the possibilities for surveillance have grown exponentially. Information systems act as social architecture, compelling participation in surveillant relationships—some desirable and others undesirable, some enabling and others constraining. Devices such as cell phones can be thought of as "polyvalent" in that they lend themselves to multiple uses, open us to multiple forms of observation and control, and position us as agents who can monitor others—for instance, when we keep track of our friends or family members.

Given this complexity, we can't simply say that surveillance is positive or negative. But that doesn't mean we're incapable of evaluating the effects of different forms of surveillance in particular contexts. That's exactly what we're encouraging you to do. Furthermore, it's also important to keep an eye on large-scale transformations in social architecture and in social practices so that we can say something about whom the systems work for and against. Technologies are never neutral. Just as the staircase creates a convenient pathway for some people but discriminates against those who can't climb stairs, surveillance architecture creates frequently hidden dynamics of inclusion and exclusion. As we proceed through the coming chapters, we'll trace some of the larger trends in how surveillance systems sort people and treat them differently based on their backgrounds or their perceived value or risk.

2: It's in the Cards

5812 5813 5921 7273 7297 7995 5933 9223 8111

Sad isn't it? An embarrassment of human decadence captured forever in the archives of the surveillance society. These damning four-digit numbers are merchant category codes that banks use to monitor and record the types of businesses where we use our credit cards. In the story told here, they are

5812 Eating places, restaurants
5813 Drinking places
5921 Package stores—beer, wine, liquor
7273 Dating escort services
7297 Massage parlors
7995 Betting/casino gambling
5933 Pawnshops
9223 Bail and bond payments
8111 Legal services, attorneys

Using these codes, card issuers and other analysts can reconstruct profiles of human behavior—a pattern of spending like this indicates high-risk behavior that could trigger an increased interest rate, a lower credit rating, or reduced credit limit.[1] In some cases, credit card companies have noticed that someone is visiting dubious businesses, reduced the credit limit below the current account balance, then charged the cardholder fees for exceeding the limit![2]

This is just one example of how the many cards we use both track what we do *and* shape the possibilities and conditions of our lives. Whether it's a credit or debit card, a student ID card, or a driver's license, our little bits of plastic are keys to different portals of the surveillance society. And just like the key card you use to open a dormitory or hotel room door, they leave a precise record of activity—where you go, when you're there, and frequently what you do. But they do more than just keep tabs. After all, "keys" open only certain doors. One of the main things we'll explore in this chapter is how these records live on to shape our lives by affecting things like our credit rating, employment prospects, and insurance rates.

We'll start with a quick look at some of the most widely used cards. Along with a basic overview of how the cards work, we'll also cover some of the policy controversies and surveillance implications surrounding different types of cards. Next we'll get to know some relatively hidden but absolutely critical institutions behind the systems of cards, data, and identities: credit-reporting agencies and data aggregators. Overall, we'll be arguing that the current system is a mess of different cards, agencies, corporations, and protocols. We believe it will soon give way to a more unified and comprehensive system of identity management and behavior monitoring. But for now, let's meet the cards.

Cards on the Table

It was an odd request from a professor: "What cards do you carry?" Sensing a chance to delay the start of a lecture, the students started digging. Everyone had a driver's license, a student ID card, a debit or credit card, and a collection of customer loyalty cards. Several had Red Cross donor cards, health insurance cards, and workplace identification cards. A few had local library cards, American Automobile Association cards, video rental cards. Some of the younger students carried fake IDs to get them into the local bars (more on this later).

We need these cards to get through many of the transactions that define our lives—working, driving, shopping, banking, and learning. And they're among the most practical, widely used, and necessary forms of surveillance in our daily lives. In most situations, cards register our presence and certify that we are who and what we say we are. A driver's license certifies that we're registered and (officially) qualified to drive and, in the United States at least, serves as a universal form of personal identification. A student or workplace ID certifies legitimate presence in an organization and frequently serves as a swipe card for accessing places or services. A debit or credit card can be coupled with a PIN (personal identification number) or signature to let us spend (or borrow) money. A customer loyalty card sometimes qualifies shoppers for discounts while providing merchants with in-depth information about purchasing histories and preferences.

The cards themselves are small—roughly 2⅛ by 3¼ inches—but their impact is huge. As each card enables access or registers our presence, it both uses and builds on a growing body of information about the cardholder. In this sense the cards are crucial tools in a complex system of digital commerce and governance. At the same time, the cards we carry are odd and increasingly antiquated throwbacks to a set of technologies that no longer match today's demands for mobility, identification, and exchange. They have two central weaknesses. First, we have so many. Second, most of them are not adequately secured against identify theft, fraud, and other forms of misrepresentation.

Because of the haphazard development of our system, we carry separate cards for our various identities (video renter, blood donor, driver, shopper, student, etc.). While there is some merging of these functions when, say, your driver's license serves as verification for banking, we have tended to keep the activities separate. This may change soon. Even though there's great political opposition to the launch of single multiuse cards, experiments are under way to explore the possibility of fusing our cards into one universal ID that could serve as everything from a driver's license to a donor card to a customer loyalty card to a video rental card. Later in this chapter we'll suggest that we may already have a lot of the features of a single card system, since companies called data aggregators gather and analyze much of what we do with our cards. You may not have heard of Experian, ChoicePoint, or Acxiom, but these profitable corporations do a good business merging data sets and reselling our profiles to others. In the process, they unify and organize the various bits of our lives to create the sort of comprehensive surveillance framework we would expect from a universal identification and access system.

The other weird thing about our current card system is just how loose and unrefined we are in our approach to identification and verification. Much of the problem is that we use cards at all! The cards merely create an increasingly obsolete plastic surrogate for each of us. To realize how strange this is, just imagine how simple it would be if we used one universal access marker such as an iris scan, a palm print, or an implanted radio-frequency identification (RFID) chip. With a central identity and access clearinghouse regulating the various transactions, a single marker could take care of receiving a speeding ticket, giving you access to rooms, taking attendance in class, spending your money, tracking your grocery purchases, and explaining your medical history and insurance coverage (whether you're conscious or not). Our cumbersome and unreliable walletful of plastic would be obsolete when replaced by a nondetachable, universal identification marker and a means of translating and implementing the various transactions and exchanges. (Of course, all new technologies create new risks: just ask the guy who lost his finger when thieves in Malaysia chopped it off to bypass the fingerprint-scan security system on his Mercedes!)[3]

Depending on where you live, the next wave of the future may already be in operation. The Baja Beach Club in Barcelona already gives bikini-clad customers the option of paying for drinks by scanning RFID chips implanted in their arms.[4] Another example is in the retail use of BioPay's small digital fingerprint scanner, which allows customers to pay for purchases directly out of their bank accounts. As BioPay president Tim Robinson said, "Kids growing up now can't imagine that you needed a cord to use your telephone. Soon they're going to say, 'You mean you have to carry around a piece of plastic or a piece of paper to go buy something?'"[5] ATM users around the world use fingerprint or finger vein scanners, while more and more bank patrons can access cash with the blink of an eye.[6] Obviously, hype typically precedes technological change, and the companies mentioned here have a vested interest in convincing all of us that their vision of the future is inevitable. We're not quite sure where things are going to end up. Even if there's a good chance that the near future will be card-free as we move into a world of iris or finger scans,[7] our plastic is an essential part of getting around and doing everything from shopping to driving to banking. In the next several pages, we go through a brief overview of the main cards we live by.

The Cards We Carry

You Are What You Eat: Customer Loyalty Cards

Food panics have become a regular part of modern life. When *E. coli* or salmonella pops up, the media get excited, federal investigators set out to find the culprit, and sometime later we learn that spinach, green onions, cantaloupe, or ground beef was to blame. But in 2009 and 2010, the storyline changed.[8] When 252 people came down with a similar strain of salmonella, investigators began with the standard approach of interviewing patients about their shopping and eating, then turned to a new idea: their supermarket shopper cards. The story was reported in *USA Today* and other news outlets, based on the statements of food-borne illness investigator Dr. Casey Behravesh:

The first case in this salmonella outbreak was reported last summer, and by November, CDC [Centers for Disease Control and Prevention] investigators were examining a multistate cluster of cases. Through interviews and questionnaires, investigators suspected some kind of Italian meat was the culprit, but people couldn't remember what brand they bought. . . . So the CDC asked supermarkets for certain buying information on seven victims in Washington State, focusing on suspect products rather than everything the customers had bought, Behravesh said. "We didn't care about the brand of toilet paper people were buying," she said.

Of those seven people, five had bought Italian meats made by the Rhode Island company, Danielle International Inc., Behravesh said. Further investigation—including the use of data from other victims' shopper cards—pointed to salami made by Danielle and, more specifically, the imported pepper it was coated in. That came from two spice suppliers in New York and New Jersey. All three companies have since recalled some products. The CDC would not say how many patients gave access to their accounts or were asked to do so, but Behravesh said most agreed.[9]

Most of us have shopper cards for our favorite larger retail, drug, and grocery stores. From a customer's perspective, they are necessary to get sale prices, which is, of course, a coercive technique on the part of stores. From the store's perspective, loyalty cards provide valuable data on customers' behavior: who buys, what they buy, what other things they buy, where they live, and what they pay.[10] This information helps stores market more effectively. With a full knowledge of shopping patterns, they can lower the price on some items (potato chips, for example) while maintaining or raising the prices on others (beer, hot dogs, and onion dip). Or they can give a price break on infant formula while raising the price on disposable diapers. They can do this because they've been able to study thousands of shoppers to explore trends in who buys what.

As they do their work, the customer cards create a wealth of data regarding the behavior of shoppers in general and specific shoppers like us. By now, somewhere between 75 and 85 percent of households use customer loyalty cards, and for most of us they've moved into the category of things we don't even think about. But there are people out there who do think about these things, and they're worried.[11] Criticism of loyalty cards takes a number of forms. Some have raised concerns about the (mis)use of specific information. For instance, when Robert Rivera shattered his kneecap when he slipped and fell in a Vons supermarket in Los Angeles, he decided to sue, only to have the store threaten to use loyalty card data to reveal how frequently he purchased alcohol.[12] It's also easy to imagine police, health insurers, or employers getting excited about access to information about all the stuff you buy. You can even find your shopping records turned over to federal investigators in the hunt for terrorists.[13]

Others worry about tipping the balance in the aggregate business-customer relationship. Without knowing who a particular customer is, retailers can use loyalty cards to develop a very sophisticated understanding of retail patterns. When unsuspecting customers move through the store, unaware that the pricing and location of products is a fine science based on careful scrutiny of behavior patterns, a form of power is at work. Manipulating consumers is an age-old game—but what are the implications of moving one side (the retailer's) into an advanced realm of retail science? It seems clear that there's more to come on this front. In some stores, advertising displays can track your eye movements to see what you focus on and for how long.[14] Other displays attempt to use facial recognition technology to keep track of the sex and race of shoppers who scrutinize goods. Through customer loyalty cards, stores already know what you buy. It's probably just a matter of time before stores use facial recognition and related systems to augment these data by tracking your unique shopping movements and susceptibility to ads.

Make Some Noise!
It may not be practical to opt out of loyalty card schemes, because we'd end up paying more for things. But there are clearly problems of power asymmetry here, where stores and data aggregators know a ton about us, but most of us have little clue what happens to our information—who owns it, whom they sell it to, or what they might do with it later on. One creative response is

to swap cards with others, even total strangers, so the data get all messed up! You still get the discounts, but the stores are foiled in their goal of collecting fine-grained, individualized data—instead they just get "noise," the technical term for data that lack any meaning. There are online card-swapping programs, card-swapping parties, or even card duplication, which can flood the system with random data when dozens—or hundreds—of people use the same card bar code.[15] (Of course, these noise-making forms of resistance could also make it harder for the CDC to discover the cause of the next outbreak of salmonella.)

Other consumer surveillance systems being piloted include a smart cart or Giving Cart[16] that offers customers a shopping cart with a card swipe and a customized presentation of coupons and location-specific shopping advice based on their past purchases. This cart will even generate a shopping list based on your past behavior. Even better, as it moves through the store, the Giving Cart can trigger commercials for products on the shelves in front of you and report to the grocer valuable information about the time you spend in each section. As the manufacturer boasts,

Other future software features of the Giving Cart™ device will include a store directory, product locator, electronic coupons, seasonal promotions, recipes, and the ability for a customer to order pharmacy and deli items on the device and be alerted (on the device) when they are ready for pickup. Other features will include system-generated shopping lists based on consumers' prior purchase histories, access to nutritional information, news items, local weather, inventory information and the ability to programmatically display a daily or weekly contest (Chime-Time feature) where customers have a chance to win gift certificates. Each wireless device is linked via the Internet to a host application. This application enables retailers, manufacturers, and third-party service providers to communicate updated content to shoppers.[17]

As we've explained, we expect plastic cards to become a thing of the past as more reliable biometric forms of identification take their place. Imagine entering your grocery store and taking a cart. The cart handle reads your fingerprints, eyes, or perhaps an RFID chip embedded in your arm. Your customer history and preferences are accessed by the onboard control system, and a host of customized offers and reminders come up on the screen. Your regular shopping list appears, with reminders about prescriptions along with tips about which wine goes well with the trout you just purchased and maybe a warning that too much pastry is a bad idea. You could even get a coupon for a bottle of chardonnay or some celery sticks. We also expect each product in the store to have an inexpensive RFID tag affixed so you simply load up the cart and leave, with the prices scanned as you exit the building with your filled cart. Good-bye "Paper or plastic?" And it's not just the bags. Expect paper money to slowly disappear as electronic transfers become the norm—for more on that, we turn to bank cards.

"Credit or Debit?"

Bank cards are like little magic wands. They allow us to withdraw or borrow cash, purchase goods and services, and rent cars or hotel rooms. Magazine ads tell us we can't really enjoy life without a credit card, and the billion-plus cards circulating in the United States alone must mean an awful lot of us are exercising our right to the pursuit of happiness.[18]

A credit card is essentially a renewing loan fund in which each expenditure borrows the needed money from the bank. If you pay the bill before the due date, no interest is charged and you've got a convenient, low-cost means of short-term financial management. But miss the due date (or, worse, a bunch of them) and the bills pile up as high interest couples with late fees. It can cost you big time. The average credit card debt for all US households is about $5,000, but if you cut out the prompt payers to look at the average among households with any card debt at all, it jumps to about $16,000. And that $16,000 is compounding at interest rates that are typically about 14 percent.[19] (In 2012, that's about four times the rate you might pay for a mortgage on a house!) Debit cards, on the other hand, don't involve a loan. They give you access to funds you already have in the bank, sometimes for a fee. Both types of cards—but particularly the credit card—tie in to an immensely important and powerful system of financial surveillance. The finance industry tracks transactions, purchases, payments, missed payments, the number of cards you hold, and almost every other facet of your credit card use and financial behavior.

One of the most familiar dimensions of financial surveillance in America is the widely used credit rating or credit score assigned to individuals by a trio of companies known as Equifax, Experian, and

TransUnion. Data are constantly gathered on how many cards, loans, and accounts you have; your total debt; your payment history; and any bad debts, bounced checks, debit card overdrafts, or consistently low balances in your checking account. All these data are gathered by the three companies, who then generate a composite score, usually called a FICO (rhymes with psycho). Scores range from 300 to 850, with the median in the low 700s.

Your credit score is used in a lot of places where you might expect it to be. When bankers decide to issue a credit card, mortgage, student loan, or car loan, they check the credit report to gauge your reliability. So do automobile dealers, retail stores, and other lenders. And the credit score is not just used to decide about the loan or the line of credit on your card; it also helps set the interest rate, since the lenders make a higher-risk person pay more for the loan. (Irony alert: Have money trouble? Low credit rating? They charge you *more* to borrow money.)

Who else uses your credit score? Some landlords use it to see if you're worthy to rent their studio apartment.[20] Potential employers use it to see how reliable you are (though legal restrictions apply). This was an especially frustrating realization for people who lost their jobs or homes during the recent "great recession" and were disqualified from new jobs because they had low credit scores. Utility and cable companies routinely run credit checks before signing customers up for services. Car insurance companies use it because they've found a strong correlation between low credit scores and high accident claim rates—for some reason that isn't fully explained, people who are higher credit risks allegedly cost insurance companies more money, so they're charged more.[21]

These examples reveal some of the control dimensions of financial surveillance. It's not just about passively collecting information. Instead, a variety of companies, employers, and landlords actively make decisions based on your financial data, and these decisions can make your life significantly harder—or easier—depending on how "risky" others think you are.

Credit Check

It might be a hassle, but you should probably take the time to review your credit report. Not only can you see where you stand; you can review it for errors and possibly detect early signs of identity theft if you discover you've unknowingly been buying auto parts in Yucatán. Free annual access to all three of your credit reports is guaranteed under the US Fair Credit Reporting Act. Keep an eye out for crafty businesses posing as the best source for credit reports. The only authorized site for online access is annualcreditreport.com. Get more information at http://www.ftc.gov/freereports.

A variation on the bank cards discussed here is the Electronic Benefit Transfer (EBT) card used for accessing food (and welfare) assistance. The same large banks, such as Citibank, run the EBT systems and often collect massive service charges from the people who have the least.[22] The older system of food stamps was somewhat anonymous—the stamps were like cash and could be traded for diapers, rent, or other things. But EBT cards let caseworkers, financial companies, and others scrutinize every purchase so that recipients can be called on to justify their purchases or be cut from assistance programs.[23] This intense scrutiny doesn't mesh well with the realities of people receiving assistance, who might, for instance, let babysitters use the card as a form of payment. Research on financial management in lower-income households shows that this sort of autonomy is a critical tool—but with the EBT cards, the tool is gone.

One of the most important things to know about credit, debit, and EBT cards is that they are not cash. Cash, like old-fashioned food stamps, leaves no trail. We don't know who had it, what they did with it, or where they did it. Plastic leaves trails: cardholder identity, items or services purchased, amount paid, location, date and time of sale. In fact, we frequently tell our students that using cash is one of the most effective ways to reduce the surveillance in their lives. But as cash becomes less and less usable with the rise of online purchasing and automated checkouts, the space for the unwatched economy gets smaller and smaller.

ID Cards

Identification is the starting point of surveillance.   —DAVID LYON[24]

Reliable identification is a constant of human life. We use facial features to recognize friends and family, phone numbers to identify the source of incoming calls, and names to trace the senders of e-mails and other messages. These sorting systems are implicitly both inclusionary and exclusionary—we're letting some people in and keeping others out. Identification is far simpler in cultures and settings where most people know each other. Imagine a small town or even your own home, where you can easily monitor for strangers as you move through the day. But now imagine San Francisco or Tokyo, or picture yourself as a border officer attempting to figure out if a prospective entrant should be approved. Here things get trickier because we need to rely on impersonal methods for identifying and sorting as we attempt to regulate movement, control access, and administer the distribution of resources.

If you've used a contemporary student identification card, you've got a pretty good idea how a comprehensive multi-use national identification card might work. Campus life has so many needs for ID cards that many students carry theirs on lanyards—as the promotional material quoted in this box demonstrates, the cards need to be ready for just about anything:

ID Badges for Everything

- A new student comes in, and while their paperwork is being filled out, an ID card is printed. This ID card has a full color picture of the student, their signature, and a barcode or magnetic stripe.
- The student visits the library and since their ID card also works as a library card, it is scanned to record the checkout details.
- The student visits the cafeteria, and instead of handing over money, they simply have their ID card scanned. Since it also works as a meal card, the total amount is deducted directly from their student account.
- The student attempts to enter the staff lounge and is unable to . . . because their special student ID card also works as a security card, and it does not allow them access to the staff lounge.
- When the student enters a classroom, they swipe their ID and are marked present. When they leave the classroom, they swipe again to verify they were in class the full time . . . and to verify where they were last. If that student turns up missing, the school's security system will know where they were last—and when.
- The student goes to computer class, and swipes their ID to log into a computer. That computer then allows access to specific applications only . . . based on their pre-set configured access levels.

These same ID cards can be used for faculty and staff.[25]

As we see here, one card is able to handle finance, access, identification, and registration. For convenience, it's hard to beat. A big risk, of course, is that so much power is invested in a single card that lacks some sort of direct biometric verification. With the current technology, a student's friend could presumably swipe the card for attendance while the student sleeps cozily in their dorm room. Without some link to a fingerprint scan or other independent verification system, multi-use identification cards have this key vulnerability.

Student ID cards also permit some interesting forms of surveillance. University officials may be able to monitor what food you buy, how often you use the gym, how steady your class attendance is, and how late you return to your dorm room. With a few data runs, they can also determine who your friends are—based on whom you enter buildings with, take attendance with, eat with, and so on.

Of course, even people who don't live on college campuses are part of identification card systems. In the United States and Canada, the driver's license is the most widely used form of government-approved identification. It usually has name, address, license number, sex, hair color, height, weight, eye color, birth date, and signature. Your license will also, typically, have information on what types of vehicle you may operate, when your license expires, whether you are an organ donor, and in some states your citizenship. There's a good chance that there's also a scannable bar code, a security hologram, and a machine-readable zone (MRZ)—the dark strip on the back.

Fake ID: Viva la Resistance?

Since 1984, when the US government compelled states to raise the legal drinking age to twenty-one, lots of people younger than twenty-one have used fake IDs to buy alcohol or get into bars. In colleges and university towns, underground economies produce new fake IDs and circulate existing ones. These fakes almost certainly wouldn't get by a police officer or border agent, but for a liquor store clerk or a halfhearted bouncer in a dark bar, they usually do the trick. But let's take a close look at what this trick is and what its implications may be.

We've already established that one of the principal needs of a surveillance society is the reliable identification of individuals. Efforts to trick identification systems produce some of the central conflicts and enforcement problems of our times; just consider the widespread attention to identity theft, the quest for the perfect biometric certifier on identification cards, or, of course, the use of fake IDs. We usually think of using fake IDs as just a relatively minor crime perpetrated by millions of people a year. But let's push this a bit and see where it takes us. Could it be that, along with being a widespread form of petty crime, fake IDs should also be thought of as a new type of political action in the surveillance society?

Fake IDs as politics? Bear with us. The drinking age isn't an act of nature; it's a political choice enacted by politicians and enforced by government agents. Around the world, some nations have no drinking age, others come in at sixteen, while others cluster between nineteen and twenty-one. Others simply ban alcohol altogether, as the United States attempted to do from 1920 to 1933. We bring up all this variance in alcohol policy to raise the point that regulations on alcohol are political choices about public policy over which there is great controversy.

A twenty-year-old who uses a fake ID to violate current regulations challenges the choices the government has made. She acts out her opposition to the official drinking age by engaging in a time-honored practice of evasion and subterfuge intended to undermine the enforcement of the law. This is a crime. But it is also an expression of a human choice to disagree with the rules of the state. This is not to say she belongs on the same moral or intellectual plane as Henry David Thoreau, Mahatma Gandhi, or Martin Luther King Jr. But it is nonetheless an action that holds political meaning.

Another dimension of the politics of fake IDs is that they challenge the identification practices of the surveillance and verification system itself. ID cards are one of the central ways governments certify and monitor the citizenry. Governments all over the world invest a great deal of time and energy into creating reliable, verifiable, and effective mechanisms of identification. When we choose to challenge them by using unsanctioned alternatives, we undermine what may be one of the principal systems of regulation and control. In these ways, odd as it may seem, there are political dynamics swirling around that twenty-year-old who may just be trying to enjoy a beer.

Government ID cards also contain at least one type of biometric data. Biometric data consist of information related to measurable physical characteristics that can then be used to identify the individual in question—like fingerprints, a photograph, or digital scans of the iris (the colored part of your eye). Considered the most accurate and consistent biometric measurement, iris scans are becoming much more popular. They have been installed on US military bases and correctional facilities and in airports all over the world, and they're even being used in place of a penthouse key at one swanky Boston hotel.[26]

Real ID?

When you think of all the things we use government ID cards for (travel, age and identity verification, check cashing), it's amazing that we don't have a better system for issuing and coordinating them. There are nationally issued passports designed for international travel, but fewer than a third of Americans have one. In the United States, state-issued driver's licenses effectively stand in for national ID cards. In 2005, the US Congress tried to clean up the confusion by passing the Real ID Act. This would have created a de facto national ID card by requiring all fifty states to adopt similar formatting, documentation, and verification standards in their state licensing and identification cards. The act also required each state to share all identification information and driving records with all other states.[27]

The response was vehement. States and organizations filed lawsuits on many grounds; legislatures voted to have their states refuse to comply. Libertarians and civil libertarians opposed Real ID. Some evangelical Christian groups contended that Real ID would be "the mark of the beast" that would usher in the apocalypse. As the politics shifted, the deadlines for compliance were extended and a prominent opponent of the plan was placed in charge of implementation. Because of the unexpectedly negative reaction, in 2009 Congress introduced Pass ID, which promised to take into account the concerns voiced about the previous plan. While some have praised the proposed changes, others see it as little more than a rebranding.[28]

National ID cards haven't fared well in other countries either. For instance, the UK government passed an Identity Cards Act in 2006 to establish a national ID card and link it to a database called the National Identity Register. But even though the United Kingdom, especially England, is said to be the most surveilled state in the world, the national identity card was repealed in 2010 with the arrival of a new coalition government (of Conservatives and Liberal Democrats). It's interesting that the coalition government could agree on this matter, most likely because conservatives thought the ID card scheme cost too much and liberals thought it invited too much abuse of civil liberties. It remains to be seen what will be done with the data already stockpiled in the UK National Identity Register.[29]

Is Real ID the Real Issue?

"Red herrings" are salted and smoked fish used to distract hunting dogs by creating a false trail. Is the ID card controversy a "red herring" in surveillance debates? After all, if our attention is focused on something like the Real ID controversy while tracking capabilities, data banks, data-mining technologies and other less visible transformations continue unnoticed, aren't we missing the more important concern? Consider all the types and forms of surveillance covered in this book, then ask yourself if an ID card is the biggest concern.

So national ID cards are having a hard time of it. This might seem puzzling. As we've seen with technologies like cell phones and credit cards, people easily embrace new surveillance. And we already live with a massive surveillance, tracking, and analysis system that fuses public and private data and allows for data mining. So why the big fuss over ID cards? Critics of national ID cards make a number of important arguments, a few of them quite relevant to our discussion here.[30] Contrary to what you might think, many analysts believe a unified national identification card compromises both our *personal* security against theft and abuse and our *national* security against something like a terrorist attack.

On the personal front, both the Real ID and the Pass ID programs create one-stop shopping for identity theft. Many security experts argue that our personal data are *more* secure when they are distributed in multiple locations, with multiple access points and multiple PINs; if we put all our eggs in the same basket, one slip can make a big mess. Under the proposed programs, personal information like your name, address, gender, age, Social Security number, and driving record would be housed on a nationally accessible state network of computers. As proposed, the system would also include digital facsimiles of critical documents such as your birth certificate or passport photo page, to be held for "at least as long as the applicable driver's license or identification card is valid." Surely great care would be taken to protect this valuable treasure of data and documents, but just as surely there would be breaches. And if data breaches worry you, *please don't read this box*:

Oops!

Lack of adequate data safeguards means big companies and government agencies are more likely to compromise your data than you are. The cases abound. In 2004 hackers broke into the database of CardSystems Solutions, gaining access to 40 million credit cards. Data aggregator ChoicePoint lost 163,000 records to criminals in the same year, leading to at least 800 documented cases of identity theft. The US Department of Veterans Affairs had personal information from 26.5 million military veterans stolen in 2006. And the Gap clothing company had a laptop stolen containing personal information for 800,000 people—names, Social Security numbers, the works. For even more scary instances like this, visit the Chronology of Data Breaches maintained by the Privacy Rights Clearinghouse: http://www.privacyrights.org/data-breach.

Shredding your bank statements won't counteract lax protection by the agencies and companies that gather, stockpile, and trade your data.[31]

United States politics goes through regular cycles of concern about border security, terrorist threats, immigration, and our interest in controlling access to the nation. National ID cards are a key part of that control effort, frequently serving as limited duty passports and offering the promise of a certain check on the identity of the bearer. National ID cards might do a great job of thwarting check fraud, but they probably wouldn't be a big help, and might even harm us, in the efforts against terrorism. This is because of the dual function of an identification card system: it keeps people out (those who lack cards), but it also lets people in (those who have cards). And as we well know, much political violence is perpetrated by citizens, who would have the cards. Further, as late-night comedians point out, suicide bombing isn't a serial crime. The perpetrators are almost always anonymous surprises who are unlikely to be recognized by an identification and tracking system. As evidence of this, all the 9/11 attackers entered the country legally with the proper visas,[32] so a robust national ID scheme wouldn't have prevented those attacks. The more we invest in a flawed solution like identification cards, the more we miss more meaningful opportunities to increase our security.

At least in the United States, our federalist system of government and a strong sense of states' rights also present ideological and financial obstacles to a national ID card. In many states there is ideological suspicion of federal laws that might alter current state practices or cede authority to federal entities. Closely coupled with these concerns are worries about the financial costs of such a system, especially if some portion of those costs is passed on to states. Together, ideological and financial obstacles played an important role in scuttling plans for a US national ID card system. But don't expect the holding pattern to go on long.

Card Tricks? Data Aggregators and Fusion Centers

ChoicePoint ... quietly amasses court rulings, tax and real estate transactions, birth and death notices. Many of these resources have existed for centuries in file cabinets and courthouse ledgers. But ChoicePoint employs an army of data collectors to harvest those facts. ... Then they put them into digital files. Files that used to exist on different pieces of paper in different buildings can now be brought together. Our profiles start to take shape, and they can glide around the world on networks.[33]

Companies like ChoicePoint, Experian, and Acxiom are data aggregators that draw on many sources to create profiles about you and sell them to those who can pay. Aggregators are the little-known overlords of the surveillance society. Driving records, credit scores, retail interests. Clothing sizes, medications, favorite cars, magazine subscriptions. Job, race, income, address. It's here, in the hands of the data aggregators, that we see the merging of the seemingly discrete worlds represented by the various cards we carry. So if you figure that your life is so disorganized, private, and fragmented that no biographer would or could keep track of it, think again—your biography is being written as you read these pages.

Through data-mining techniques, data aggregators can uncover information about us as easily as we can Google a new movie. We have different cards for the different aspects of our lives, but many of our records end up providing data that are then organized at aggregation centers, where our entire profile can be tapped through any node—a phone number, a street address, or, of course, a Social Security number. There's even a set of tricks known as "reidentification" for reattaching seemingly anonymous data to the individuals in question. So, ironically, we get all the concentration of information and control manifest in a national data system without the convenience of pruning a quarter of an inch of plastic from our daily load.

We think of our credit cards, driver's licenses, customer cards, and other means of access and identification as separate tools for separate needs. We might take comfort in the unconnected nature of these realms, having faith that a potential employer or landlord won't be able to learn about the birth control we use or the speeding tickets racked up during a run of bad luck. We may also live in the expectation that pharmaceutical purchases, automotive preferences, clothing tastes and sizes, and voting habits are all separate and largely unknowable owing to the complexity of the economy and the sheer volume of transactions.

But it just ain't so. In a private-sector surveillance system that would humble any of Big Brother's fantasies, data aggregators accumulate massive amounts of information from businesses, government agencies, and credit card companies. Profiles about us are then used to go way beyond simple things like a credit score. They can issue all sorts of reports on all types of people. Potential employers, landlords, attorneys, and bankers can get reports on your litigation history, criminal record, motor vehicle record, and workers' compensation claims.[34] Data-mining techniques allow corporations to target advertising, develop mailing lists for direct-mailing advertisers, generate contact lists for political campaigns, or pull just about any other analysis out of their massive data banks.

In the wake of September 11, 2001, when the US government sought to rapidly and massively expand its surveillance programs, these firms were happy to cooperate (in the correct expectation that large and profitable contracts would follow). In the sort of easy private-public partnership we saw when looking at law enforcement's access to cell phone tracking, data aggregators' products readily circulate in national security, law enforcement, and commercial surveillance networks.[35] Even before the 2001 attacks, InfraGard was established in 1996 as an information-sharing partnership between the FBI and the private sector. As of 2010, InfraGard boasted representatives from "350 of our nation's Fortune 500" companies and shared office space with the Los Angeles Joint Regional Intelligence Center, a fusion center that gathers data from seven counties in Southern California.[36]

Public-private partnerships have flourished since 9/11, with fusion centers serving as the government's version of data aggregators. In 2006 the Department of Justice released "Fusion Center Guidelines" stressing the importance of integrating the private sector into the intelligence-gathering process and giving multiple examples of the information or technical help each sector could provide. Boeing, for example, has a full-time company intelligence analyst stationed at the Seattle Fusion Center, while Microsoft helped create software necessary to integrate the information stored in the Massachusetts database. One issue raised by these arrangements is that corporate personnel might be able to tap information not readily available to the general public (or to competitors of the company involved). Along these lines, Boeing executive Richard E. Hovel testified to a congressional committee that private-sector employees at fusion centers should be granted access to any classified or unclassified information about potential threats to private companies.[37]

We see here that traditional distinctions between government and industry are rapidly blurring. When the government needs data mining, it turns to the data aggregators; when the FBI needs a new generation of surveillance technology, it calls Lockheed Martin; when a school adds an ID card system, it shops out the job to a competitive industry of surveillance practitioners. When data aggregators want to know about your legal history and marital status, they go to the courthouse. And when credit-reporting companies make declarations about your life, they implement rules and wield power as forcefully as any government agency. But at a broader level, the fusion of public and private institutions is even more profound. For we are witnessing the emergence and perfection of a system of human regulation that uses identification, visibility, and surveillance as its central strategies. In that process, all significant institutions are implementing similar models of governance. Colleges and universities, banks, data aggregators, grocers, state governments, insurers, police departments, the FBI, and so on—they're all committed to practices of management and control that rely on gathering and acting on detailed information about our lives.

Conclusion

A close inspection of the cards in your wallet or purse—or wrapped in a rubber band in your pocket—can crack open a whole new dimension of the surveillance society. Cards are tokens that can identify you, give you access to money or locations, track your purchases and provide discounts, allow you to cross certain borders, or let you receive health care. They may be a necessary mechanism for people to deal with problems of trusting strangers—the card verifies that you are who you say you are or that you're good for it, whatever "it" is.

Cards also generate massive amounts of fine-grained information about you, your habits, your preferences, and your risks. For some, like customer loyalty cards, this is their sole purpose; the discounts are just an afterthought, giving you an incentive to comply. When data aggregators get hold of all this personal information, they can spin a dense web of surveillance with no place to hide. It's not some evil Orwellian plan—it's just the normal operation of modern bureaucracies and capitalist systems. Regardless, the resulting surveillant assemblage is not infallible or unbiased. A mistake on your credit report could haunt you for a long time, and if you're deemed especially risky, you can be discriminated against even if you didn't do anything wrong. If you were born into or somehow found yourself in serious financial distress, the possibilities for rebuilding or starting over are now very limited. These invisible surveillance systems, in other words, have their own non-neutral codes and values. They deal good hands to those seen as valuable and stack the deck against those considered risky.

As we've said a couple of times, the surveillance technologies discussed in this chapter seem poised for dramatic change in the very near future. The plastic cards will probably soon seem like the cords and rotary dials on old-fashioned telephones. We're not sure what the interface will be, or if there will even be one—it could be your eyeball or fingerprint that gets scanned. But one thing is clear, the currently sloppy linkages between the identification of individuals and the knowledge stored about them will be tightened as technological, administrative, and financial capacities and imperatives advance. The pieces are nearly in place for the mother of all fusion centers to unite our medical, personal, financial, legal, and other identities into one seamless searchable system. We don't think this fusion will spring from some grand declaration or congressional act. We think it will come out of the quieter cooperative meshing of public- and private-sector initiatives.

3: Lives Online

- Facebook users outside the United States have been using their information rights to see what Facebook knows about them. The result: over 1,200 pages of data for one person, including old chats, pokes, and material that had been deleted years before.[1]
- A search-engine user wanted to know more about her town's supply of single men over sixty. She hardly expected her private query to appear in the newspaper. Her dating prospects weren't helped when the newspaper also reported on her search for how to deal with her dog's tendency to pee on everything.[2]
- The online dimension of our lives is becoming so important that new firms are popping up to help us manage and enhance online reputations, while others help employers and lawyers dig up any dirt we may have left in the worlds of Facebook, Twitter, or anything Google can find.[3]

The Internet facilitates communication, fosters creative expression, and opens quick and convenient access to troves of information. With our computers and mobile devices, we can just look up whatever it is we need to know: a good restaurant, directions to the department of motor vehicles, the number for the nearest animal shelter, the current world population, whatever. Internet applications can also predict our interests in a rather eerie way. They do this by constantly monitoring our online behavior and profiling us so they can tell us what they think we want to know (or what advertisers want us to know). For instance, Google algorithms can track everything you search for, your location, your demographic information, and much more to give you the search results it thinks you want. Similar profiling happens with Facebook, where every time you "check in" to a physical place or "like" some news story, you give companies data they can use to construct a profile and pitch products to you.

On the one hand, that's pretty cool, right? It's nice to have some software algorithm anticipate what we want. On the other hand, the constant effort to anticipate and understand is an intensive kind of surveillance about things that can be highly personal. Do we really want strangers to know what we search for, what we post to our Facebook pages, what we say in an e-mail, and where we go on the weekend? As we'll discuss in this chapter, part of the problem with online surveillance is that there's lots of contextual spillover, which means that information people think is private, limited to a specific purpose, or intended for a select few really isn't.

Companies like Google and Facebook engage in surveillance because it's profitable. They don't want our data, pictures, preferences, friends, contacts, and personal history just because they're nosy—the information is used to design marketing campaigns and other products that are earning billions and billions of dollars. And the amazing thing is that we volunteer all this valuable information free of charge. Technically, we do agree to these practices by using these applications, but it would be hard to call it "informed consent" when most people are unaware of what's going on behind the scenes. So let's take a look.

Facebook Surveillance? But We're Just Friends!

We use a simple and widely shared definition of surveillance as *monitoring people in order to regulate or govern their behavior*. Earlier we saw that *surveillance* comes from the French words for "watch" and "above," so it's similar to more commonly used terms like *supervise* and *oversight*. Each of these combines the idea of *vision* with the *power* that distinguishes surveillance from just taking a look around. Surveillance involves power. So how is Facebook surveillance? Where's the power?

First off, as you'll soon see, Facebook is not just you and your friends. It's you and your friends, and future employers, and corporate advertisers, and law-enforcement officers, and even firms hired to dig up cyberdirt—there's a whole lot of power going on. You may not notice it right now, but it's there, and it may turn up in surprising ways at any point in your life.

Second, there are power dynamics at work even when it is just you and your friends. Friends watch friends, in part, to enact informal versions of regulation and governance. On Facebook, you decide who is included as a friend and who isn't, who is on your special list of "close friends" and who is relegated to the "acquaintance" or "restricted" lists, whose posts you like and whose you ignore, which photos you comment on and which you untag yourself from, whom you stalk and whom you block, and whom you report for posting potentially suicidal content. All of this involves the regulation of relationships and groups, and—as we're sure you know—this means power.[4]

Social Networking

How many friends do you have? If we're talking about everyone who may be tracking your posts on social networking sites such as Facebook or Twitter, the group may be much larger and more inclusive than you'd imagine. Just like using cell phones, being plugged in to online networks can be fun, addictive, convenient, mundane, and sometimes downright scary. Take Facebook. Now more than 800 *million* users share photographs, political viewpoints, personal achievements, and devastating crises with vast webs of "friends," many of whom they may never have met in person. In addition, Facebook "news feeds" and other features have become a way—and for some people the primary way—of communicating with others: letting people know what you "like," where you'll be and when, what your new phone number is, and what you think about your friends' many posts. In short, Facebook has become a compelling new medium for crafting identities and becoming part of communities. People perform in this online medium in ways that are deeply symbolic too, like when couples pause during wedding ceremonies to change their relationship status from single to married.[5]

There's also a great deal of surveillance going on—in some ways that's the whole point. People use social networking sites to see and be seen. Rather than being a prisonlike panopticon where trapped people follow the rules because they're afraid someone is watching, with Facebook and similar sites people are probably more afraid that no one is watching, that no one cares what they're up to. So, many users discipline themselves in a different way by divulging as much as possible about their lives and thoughts. In this medium, being connected means actively—and sometimes obsessively—participating, even if the content is shallow or trite.

As you might imagine, all this action leaves quite a history. For example, using the relatively strong European laws about people's rights to their own data, Max Schrems, a twenty-four-year-old Austrian law student, asked Facebook for what they had on him:

Max received a CD containing about 1,222 pages (PDF files), including chats he had deleted more than a year ago, "pokes" dating back to 2008, invitations, and hundreds of other details. . . . [These details included] the exact times Max logged in and wrote messages, the times of day [of] messages he sent or received, Max's friend network, the locations of the pictures he took in Vienna, and the most popular tags of Max's messages.[6]

It wouldn't be news to most Facebook users that there are potential downsides to these relationships of surveillance. Broadcasting so much about our lives makes it much harder to keep secrets. Day-to-day, this might mean it's hard to prevent parents, former boyfriends or girlfriends, or needy acquaintances from knowing whom we're with and where we go. Occasionally "friends" can turn out to be stalkers or identity thieves—not the sort of people who should have access to our personal information. Another potential downside is our loss of control over posted data. Most of us know, at least vaguely, that our online personas could come back to haunt us: that insulting thing you said about a classmate might not look so good when you're on a job interview ("I'm a team player") or running for public office someday ("We must return to civility"). Beer pong pics that are loads of fun when you're twenty-one won't be such a hoot when you're twenty-eight and applying for a position with a top law firm or defense contractor.

But most of us accept these downsides and provide all this information with little thought. One of the most surprising things about our emergent surveillance society is how we willingly flock to new forms of surveillance. A conventional expectation might be that the freedom-loving people of Western democracies would recoil at the totalitarian implications of corporate Big Brotherism. But no. Even though cell phones, Facebook, and Google are all highly advanced systems of surveillance, most of us eagerly throw ourselves into their arms. This raises all sorts of really interesting (and tough!) questions:

- Are people simply unaware of what they're signing up for?
- Are people fully informed, but making a quick trade-off for the convenience?

- Are we somewhat aware but willingly embracing these new technologies because they are present and seem necessary for modern life?
- Is it still surveillance when we volunteer? (Hint: yes.)

And keep an eye on how many times we let slip the word willing. To what extent are we truly willing participants when a nearly universal architecture of communication (cell phones, e-mail, Facebook, etc.) dominates our social world and becomes necessary for keeping a job, attending school, or having a life? Can you really opt out? Can you really even *imagine* opting out?

Privacy Ain't What It Used to Be

It would be complicated enough if your surveillance exposure with social networking sites were limited to your small community of chosen friends, but many prying eyes are keenly interested in the data you produce with comments and posts. Facebook may have become a successful platform because it cultivates active engagement by users, but it's become an insanely profitable company by selling user data to third parties and allowing marketers to target individuals with specially tailored advertisements. The company is not above instilling guilt in users, too: if you try to delete your account, you'll see pictures of your friends and be told how much they'll miss you when you're gone. The choice, as one commentator put it, is to "participate or fade into a lonely obscurity."[7]

Obviously, many people find the "choice" to reveal tons of personal data to unknown third-party companies or government agencies worth it for the privilege of using Facebook. As company founder and CEO Mark Zuckerberg says, "What people want isn't complete privacy. . . . [Instead] they want control over what they share and what they don't." And "the mission of the company is to make the world more open and connected."[8] Of course, Zuckerberg has also referred to Facebook users as "dumb fucks" for willingly giving his company all their personal data,[9] so we should be a bit skeptical about his utopian rhetoric of openness and connectedness. For thinking about surveillance, however, it's vital to understand that exposure to surveillance has been carefully and intentionally designed into the Facebook platform.

The gradual disintegration of Facebook's privacy protections reveals the adaptability of its "take it or leave it" platform design. For instance, in 2005 Facebook's privacy policy was fairly straightforward and robust:

No personal information that you submit to Thefacebook [which is what Facebook used to be called] will be available to any user of the Web Site who does not belong to at least one of the groups specified by you in your privacy settings.[10]

By 2009 the privacy policy read more like a lack-of-privacy policy:

Certain categories of information such as your name, profile photo, list of friends and pages you are a fan of, gender, geographic region, and networks you belong to are considered publicly available to everyone, including Facebook-enhanced applications, and therefore do not have privacy settings. You can, however, limit the ability of others to find this information through search using your search privacy settings.[11]

The deterioration of Facebook's privacy protections betrays that this medium isn't simply adapting to new conceptions of privacy as embodied by younger people—it is actively *shaping* those conceptions and slowly pushing users toward acceptance of further exposure and less control.[12] The default is for users to be opted in to all kinds of data sharing and to make it difficult for them to alter their settings or even to keep up with the constantly changing options. Indeed, 23 percent of Facebook users either don't know about privacy controls or don't use them.[13] You don't have to be a conspiracy theorist to see this as intentional. The design of the system encourages users to just have fun sharing and to not worry about how others are using the data.

The Writing's on the Wall

Facebook and other social networking sites intentionally bring about two kinds of surveillance: peer surveillance of "friends" watching "friends," and marketing surveillance of companies learning what you—or people like you—want. Marketers can then tap into Facebook networks to hit you with targeted peer-pressure campaigns telling you what your friends like and encouraging you to buy those things too. This extends way beyond the Facebook site, of course. Users can now click that they "like" almost anything on the web (pizza, movies, news stories, books), and all those opinions are collected and stored and tied to your profile. These expressions of identity are also broadcast to your news feed for all your friends to see in real time. The same function now exists for most social networking applications. It is also accessible through mobile devices, so you can amass tons of data points and expose yourself to monitoring from almost anywhere.

So if younger people care more about control than privacy, as Facebook's Mark Zuckerberg claims, how much control do you think you have over your data? What you broadcast to the world has the potential to be "out there" forever. Even if you take the radical step of deleting your Facebook account, you can't erase information you shared with others. You may also not be able to purge data that have already been distributed to third-party websites or applications. And on occasion Facebook has both intentionally and unintentionally made its users' personal information available to all search engines—and therefore to everyone—on the web, so there may be a lot of your material out "in the wild." Moreover, the Facebook privacy policy states that even if you delete your account (a step beyond merely deactivating it), the company "may retain certain information," but the policy doesn't say what that information is, how long they'll retain it, or who gets to use it.[14] So much for control. But wait, there's more.

In 2007 a couple of students at MIT were able to concoct a basic algorithm for figuring out which Facebook users were homosexual.[15] They named it Gaydar. Even if people had not indicated it in their profiles, it was relatively easy to accurately predict someone's sexual orientation just by counting how many gay friends that person had. A few statistical operations later, and voilà, people could be "outed" without even knowing it. This basic function extends beyond discovering who is or isn't gay, though. By adding information from a person's profile and looking at someone's friends, researchers could also predict a Facebook user's religion, age, and political affiliation. So, even if we think we're in control and are careful about not disclosing sensitive information, our associations could foil our efforts to manage the identity we project to the world.

It's Easier than You'd Think

Even companies that care about protecting users' privacy can have a difficult time doing so. The popular DVD-delivery and movie-streaming company Netflix, for instance, had the brilliant idea of creating a contest where computer scientists or others could win $1 million for improving the company's movie recommendation system.[16] For this contest, Netflix designed a special database that was stripped of all personal identifiers (through "de-identification") and made that database available to contestants. It didn't take long for two researchers at the University of Texas to reidentify the anonymous data by comparing movie ratings in Netflix's database with movie ratings on the Internet Movie Database (IMDb.com). They then were able to name customers, know what they watched, and know what their ratings were. Because this violated the company's privacy policy, Netflix was investigated by the Federal Trade Commission and sued. The contest was discontinued.

You're probably more than aware that parents, campus security officers, and employers can scour social networking sites and crack down on things they don't like. In 2010 Ashley Johnson was waiting tables at Brixx Wood Fired Pizza in Charlotte, North Carolina, when she found out the hard way that she shouldn't complain about customers on Facebook. Even though her privacy settings were limited to friends who didn't work at the pizza place, she was fired for venting about two customers who kept her an hour after her shift and didn't tip well.[17] She has no idea how the company found out.

Did you know that insurance companies are watching people on Facebook too? In one remarkable case, a Canadian woman who was on long-term disability because of clinical depression lost her sick-leave benefits when an insurance agent found pictures that seemed to show her having a good time. Her insurance company told her the Facebook pictures were "evidence that she is no longer depressed."[18] What's somewhat crazy about this is that a clinical diagnosis made by a licensed physician is trumped by an insurance agent who equates smiling with the absence of depression. The message is that Facebook evidence can and will be used against you. Read on to see how sharing something with your friends can have major legal consequences.

Maxi Sopo committed bank fraud in Seattle, then fled to Mexico. There he made a grave mistake when he posted (to "friends" only) that he was having a good time across the border. His settings may have been private, but his friends' settings were not, so agents were able to locate Sopo and have Mexican authorities nab him for extradition to the United States.[19] FBI agents are also busy creating false online profiles to communicate with suspects, view all their postings and photographs, and try to lure them into admitting wrongdoing.[20] Sometimes agents even impersonate a suspect's friend or family member. This would be illegal in the physical world but, as you know, just about anything goes on the Internet.

We expect to see a lot more dredging up of online behavior, since many legal systems allow parties involved in a lawsuit to subpoena records they think pertain to the case, even those held by a third party such as Facebook. This can sometimes be a mortifying surprise to people. For instance, when an electrical fire at Wal-Mart severely burned Disa Powell's husband and brother and they chose to sue, the company subpoenaed *her* Facebook and MySpace accounts for all data going back two and a half years. There were pictures of Powell's newborn baby lying in a hospital bed after heart surgery ("The hardest day of Mommy and Daddy's life") and messages detailing problems with her pregnancy ("I got a bladder infection, which has moved to my kidneys").[21]

Understandably, Disa Powell was embarrassed and angry that her private information was revealed. According to the attorney for her husband and brother, that's precisely the point: more and more, corporations and others are employing subpoenas to "discover information that would be embarrassing . . . even if it has nothing to do with the claim."[22] When information is posted on social networking sites, those sites own it. Thus these companies willingly comply with legal requests in order to protect themselves, not their users.

The examples reviewed so far show that in addition to surveillance by peers and by advertisers, social networking opens people up to all kinds of unwanted scrutiny. We can think of these alternative forms of monitoring as instances of "function creep"—what happens when technological systems expand beyond their original purposes. The creators of Facebook probably didn't plan on designing platforms that would encourage parents to spy on their children, employers to fire their employees, FBI agents to track suspects, insurance companies to deny medical benefits, gay people to be involuntarily outed, or corporations to humiliate the families of litigants. That the systems are being used for these purposes means that we have to include both intended *and* unintended outcomes in our analysis. Technologies are dynamic entities, which is one reason they can be so exciting. But the dynamics of unintended consequences mean that by participating in social networking, we are much more transparent to others and have much less control over our information than we would like to believe.

Library of Tweets?

In 2010 the US Library of Congress announced, through a text message "tweet," that it would be archiving *all* Twitter messages, from 2006 into the future. Every short burst of text, whether by President Obama or the kid down the street, will now be stored indefinitely, available for everyone to scrutinize. On the library's official blog, Matt Raymond reflected on this decision: "It boggles my mind to think what we might be able to learn about ourselves and the world around us from this wealth of data. . . . And I'm certain we'll learn things that none of us now can even possibly conceive."[23]

Foursquare Dance

Some of the breakthrough applications in social networking operate at the intersection of virtual and physical worlds. For instance, "Foursquare," a widely popular application, allows people to use their smartphones to "check in" at physical locations. When you indicate where you are in physical space, such as a bar or a club, your friends can come and join you without asking the cell phone cliché "Where are you now?" One possible unanticipated consequence of checking in everywhere is that you're telling people when you're not home, so someone might rob your house or apartment without any awkward interruptions.

Foursquare and similar applications pitch themselves in two ways: by playing on people's fears of being alone and by providing various symbolic and monetary incentives for people to share their locations. Some of the popular stories about Foursquare start out with stressful examples of people arriving at bars or clubs and not seeing anyone they know. The user then checks in to the location using Foursquare and—at least in principle—is soon met by friends who also use Foursquare. Symbolic and monetary incentives come in the form of virtual badges, being declared "mayor" or "boss" of an establishment, finding a virtual coaster that entitles you to a free drink, getting coupons for products, or collecting points in customer loyalty schemes. Evidently these sales techniques are working, since Foursquare has more than 10 million users who are checking in about 3 million times a day.[24]

But there's a catch, and—you saw this coming—it involves surveillance. According to Dennis Crowley, one of the creators of Foursquare,

"Each time you check in, you're giving permission to share your location and get pinged with information about interesting things nearby."[25] Thus, instead of home burglary, a more commonplace outcome is that users of Foursquare and similar applications—like Loopt Star, Pulse, or Facebook Places—are generating a wealth of data for advertisers and others. Companies can take advantage of knowing your location and shopping habits to advertise to you in multiple ways. PepsiCo, for instance, has created a Foursquare-based loyalty program to send live notifications to people when they're close to stores selling Pepsi products. Since that sounds a bit too much like spam, they've made it into a game, Pepsi Loot, that allows subscribers to collect points toward "free" music downloads.[26] Starbucks, Macy's, Tasti D-Lite, and others have joined in with coupons and other incentives too.

Once companies motivate users to enter stores, their next objective is to advertise to customers while they're there and get them to buy (more) stuff. Location-based applications in development will register you, through your phone, as soon as you enter a store and ostensibly give you access to information to help you shop. "Where's the flour?" "Do you have these jeans in my size?" By signing up for services like one called Presence,[27] shoppers can also be sent real-time coupons while they're in a store and can get reminders like "Do you want to purchase sprinkles and frosting with that cake mix?" While this may be convenient for customers, it's also a marketer's dream. These applications tell companies who's checking in to their locations, how often, at what times, what they buy, whether they're men or women, their ages, where they live, and more. It's not just vague categories of potential customer profiles either—this information is fine-grained and individualized.

As with Facebook, the issue is not just taking advantage of loosening concerns about privacy to introduce profitable and convenient services. Instead, it's coaching people to be less concerned about disclosing personal information. According to a recent survey, for instance, roughly "two-thirds of Americans object to online tracking by advertisers."[28] Moreover, contrary to anecdotes suggesting that younger people are more complacent about disclosing information and being tracked, the survey found that "55 percent of respondents from [ages] 18 to 24 objected to tailored advertising."[29] Given existing concerns that people, young and old, have about invasive marketing and unwanted attention, systems of incentives and rewards are designed to coax them to acquiesce to full transparency and surveillance. According to Sam Altman, Loopt's chief executive, the plan to lower reservations is working: "People are getting more comfortable so fast [because] they see the upside is huge—run-ins with friends and cool specials."[30]

Also, the likelihood of unplanned surveillance has increased. Sometimes, as with Facebook Places, friends can check us in to places without our permission. So even if we're careful about what information we divulge, we don't have much control. But these locational surveillance applications aren't just about "run-ins with friends" who are monitoring our movements or "cool specials" from companies that are collecting data about us. When we broadcast our locations, movements, purchases, and searches to the various players on the Internet, this information can be tapped by law enforcement, insurance companies, repressive governments, homophobic employers, suspicious spouses, identity thieves, and others. We don't mean to sound alarmist; it's just a fact: the more information we give up, the more likely it is that someone will use the information in ways we don't condone. This is how function creep works. It's also important to underscore that the systems don't have to operate this way. One *could* have a social networking site built on strong principles of privacy, like the open-source Appleseed Project,[31] and one *could* have apps that connect you to friends without sending your data to advertisers.

Google

The perfect search engine would be like the mind of God.   —Google cofounder SERGEY BRIN[32]

O LORD, you have searched me and you know me. You . . . are familiar with all my ways.   —Psalm 139

People use search engines to look up all sorts of embarrassing or sensitive topics—like weird rashes in unusual places, pregnancy scares, porn, or how to fight a speeding ticket. Search engines, as you know, can sort through billions of web pages of information.[33] Just enter your search terms, and in milliseconds you've got a list of (potentially) relevant pages to help answer most questions you might have. They've made it possible for the average user to effectively navigate the Internet, and one company is even responsible for a new verb. (Just google "verb google" and you'll see what we mean.)

It's a pretty safe bet that we've all used search engines to look up embarrassing stuff and would hate to have the records of our searches pop up on the front page of the newspaper. So imagine Thelma Arnold's surprise when the *New York Times* reported that she was AOL member 4417749 and that she had been searching subjects like "60 single men" and "dog that urinates on everything." This all happened after AOL released anonymized search data in the belief that actual user identities could not be reconstructed from the data—they were wrong.[34] But the most important implications of search engines and surveillance are probably not tied to regrettable dog behavior—they are about the Google empire's control over the information.

All search engines are a bit different, but the basics are the same: computer programs called spiders search the Internet. These spiders "crawl" through the information on a website and follow every link to a new page, recording everything they find and bringing it back to the search engine. The search engine then creates a searchable index to give you the answers you need.[35] Most search engines employ algorithms that draw on user behavior to improve the results.[36] This is a useful skill in a machine, and generally a welcome one.

It does, however, raise questions regarding what kind of information is gathered in the course of the machine's self-improvement, how long the machine needs to hold on to it, and how the information is being used. Unlike social networking sites, where we intend to share information, people use search engines to research all kinds of topics they'd like to keep confidential. And search engines don't just record what you ask. They also, typically, record your computer's Internet protocol (IP) address, the sites you click on, and how long you stay there.[37] An IP address is a string of numbers assigned by the computer network you're using (think of it as a phone number). It functions just like any other address: it tells the server where to send the information you request. Together with the IP addresses being used around you (from say, a business with a WiFi connection), an IP address can also be used to identify your physical address or geographic location (with varying accuracy, of course).[38]

All the information extracted from your search (and wherever else you went without closing your browser) is written to a "cookie" the search engine sends to your computer. A cookie is a small text file initially placed in the memory of your web browser by a website you visit. When the website's server sends your browser a cookie for the first time, it designates a unique ID containing a name and a value. Cookies are used for all kinds of things, like recognizing your computer and filling in user names or passwords for you, keeping track of what's in your virtual shopping cart while you browse in an online store, pulling up credit card information, remembering user preferences (such as weather reports for a specific zip code), and determining how many people visit a particular website[39] and how often they come back.[40]

Web of the Living Dead

Even if you regularly delete cookies, some are persistent "zombie" cookies that will reanimate themselves, grab your personal information, and continue to send it to third parties or "affiliates." For example, Disney has partnered with a company called Clearspring Technologies, which uses a Flash-embedded zombie cookie to continue to report information about users, who one might expect are mostly children. The data captured can be fine-grained, including "video viewing habits, gender, age, race, education level, geographic location, sexual preference, what the users like to read, home address, phone number, health condition, and more."[41] Obviously cookies can be pretty serious stuff, and federal law limits the way federal agencies may use them on their websites. The CIA,[42] the Department of Homeland Security,[43] the National Security Agency,[44] the Office of National Drug Control Policy under Bill Clinton, as well as the Bush[45] White House have gotten into trouble for using persistent cookies on their websites.

Search engines use this information in various ways. The first, detailed above, is related to improving search-engine services for the end user—that's you. By personalizing content for users, search engines like Google give different results to different people. Thus, one person searching for "BP" at the height of the oil rig disaster in 2010 was directed to news stories about the crisis, while another person received investment links that didn't even mention the blowout.[46] In this way the fusion of search engines and online media can hide a lot of information from us by creating "filter bubbles" that prevent us from seeing or hearing things that could be very important.[47] You might live in Pennsylvania but never know that some tap water in your state is so contaminated it can catch fire right from your faucet.[48] You might never have heard of the genocide in Darfur because none of your Facebook friends dared to click that they "like" that.[49] Online surveillance performs a kind of invisible censorship by putting you inside a bubble world filled with the things it thinks you want to see.

The information collected from end users is also sold to marketing agencies that create consumer profiles and craft ads targeting certain groups. This is a huge business, as illustrated by the data aggregation giants profiled in chapter 2. It's no less important for companies like Google, which generates 96.7 percent of its total revenue from advertising companies.[50] All this marketing earned Google an incredible estimated 39 percent of all online ad revenue in 2010.[51]

Given these figures, it should be evident that an advertiser will pay big bucks to be visible to a potential customer. Take a look at a couple of numbers about Google to visualize an Internet success story: in the United States, 72 percent of all Internet searches go through Google,[52] while in some European countries the figure's about 95 percent.[53] This is how Google has become a multibillion-dollar corporation while providing completely free online services to millions of users each day. It also means that Google is making billions by keeping track of what its users are doing online so it can provide more detailed information to advertisers and more relevant ads to users.

Had Google remained the humble search engine of its early days, perhaps search-based tracking would not seem like such a big deal: all you'd have to do is delete the Google cookie and start using a different search engine (with cookies either disabled or deleted when you closed your browser). But the executives at Google didn't become billionaires by sitting on their hands for the past decade. Since 1998, Google has acquired over seventy companies and thereby has become the owner of all kinds of programs for bringing services to the masses. If Google's first goal is to make money by selling users' data to advertisers or other interested parties, its second is to figure out how to successfully collect data, and it does that by recording every step you take online.

To do this, the programmers have created software for nearly every aspect of surfing the web. Your cell phone may run Google's Android operating system, or your computer may use Google's Chrome operating system and browser. The Chrome browser collects everything you type into the navigation bar (where you put in the website address) even before you hit Enter.[54] Type in a website but decide not to go there? Google has already collected that information. Google also provides all kinds of services once you're online: e-mail, news, social networking, music, phone service, books, videos, photos, travel planning, personal health records, aerial and Street View maps, as well as software for creating documents, presentations, and websites and storing them in the cloud. Though it may feel like all these realms are carefully managed and self-contained, the more Google services you use, the more information Google has about you.

So what kind of monitoring are we talking about? Exactly what do you agree to when you click the Terms of Service box when you sign up or start to surf? We'll start with one of their most popular programs, the web-based e-mail program called Gmail (Google Mail in the United Kingdom). Remember those spiders Google uses to find and index web pages? It uses similar technology to record your interactions over Gmail (including information sent from outside, non-Gmail accounts).[55] For example, if you write an e-mail to a friend about the camping trip you're planning, Google translates that into ads for camping equipment in the margins of your account page. When you use a university- or work-issued e-mail account, those organizations are within their legal rights to monitor and read your e-mail. Universities using Gmail may not have the same total access to student and employee e-mail, because the servers are housed elsewhere and owned by Google, but they're effectively giving your personal information over to Google and its marketing partners. Indeed, these concerns led the University of California, Davis, to make a high-profile decision to reject Gmail as its campuswide system.[56]

And a Gmail account isn't limited to e-mail—you can use your log-in information for multiple Google services, some available from your Gmail home page. Google Talk is a program that supports IM (instant messaging) chats, all recorded, indexed, and searchable unless you're chatting in "off the record" mode. Google Voice is a phone service that allows you to get a single phone number capable of ringing all your phones and your computer. It supports voice-mail and text messages and can also be used for live webcam chats. Google records all the phone calls, voice-mails, or text messages you send and receive, as well as the conversations you have while signed in.[57] Your voice-mails are even transcribed (changed from voice to text) so you (and Google?) can search them![58] Your Google account is also used for Google Docs, that handy office application hosted in the cloud where one or more users can see and work on a single document, spreadsheet, presentation, drawing, or form. "In the cloud" refers to computing that is entirely Internet-based, as opposed to being stored on your computer, and all Google services are considered cloud computing.

There's great risk in trusting a single company with so much personal information. Thousands of Yahoo!, Hotmail, and Google users discovered this unfortunate fact when their log-in names and passwords were stolen and published on the Internet.[59] Should there be any security breaches, or an unethical person working at Google, significant abuses could occur. Something like this happened in 2010 when a twenty-seven-year-old site reliability engineer at Google spied on and harassed four teenagers. He read their IM chats and quoted them back to them, then accessed one boy's Google Voice log to figure out which of the girls the boy was dating. He threatened to contact her, invited the teens to the movies, and at one point "unblocked" himself after one of the kids blocked him from a Google Talk buddy list.[60] Naturally Google fired the engineer shortly after they found out about the abuses. Some of the stories reporting on this "Gcreep" pointed out the irony of Google's developing a Family Safety Center to help parents protect their children: "The biggest threat to kids' privacy might be Google employees themselves."[61]

The story about the activities of the predator working at Google could be thought of as another instance of function-creep surveillance. There are many other ways, however, that function creep can easily grow out of search engines and online apps too. Google discloses Gmail contents and search terms to authorities investigating crimes. (Advice: Don't search for "neck, snap, break, and hold" or read "22 Ways to Kill a Man with Your Bare Hands" before killing someone. Those searches can and will be used against you in a court of law.[62] Better advice: Don't kill people.) Yahoo! provided "e-mail and other account data to Chinese officials, resulting in the jailing of dissidents within that country."[63] The US Department of Justice has requested search-engine data from individuals' search terms, supposedly to crack down on online pornography; the request was honored by Yahoo!, Microsoft, and AOL.[64] While there are some anonymous proxy services available for web surfing (like one called Tor),[65] they tend to slow down one's data transfer, so even people who are aware of them often choose not to use them.

The Death of Net Neutrality?

Here's one important theme to take note of: We may be generating personal and public data in totally different places (iTunes, school, doctor's office) and for totally different purposes (entertainment, learning, communicating), but that doesn't mean these data are kept separate. More and more, they're reconnected and concentrated in the hands of a few companies, like Google. As a result our lives are much more public, we have much less control over information about us, and we're exposed to surveillance by peers, government agencies, advertisers, and others. Another outcome, though, is that the few companies that manage all these data are in a position to regulate who has access to what—and at what speeds.

This brings us to an issue known as net neutrality. The basic, original structure of the Internet is a decentralized, weblike network that allows packets of information to find the most expeditious route between sender and receiver. The Internet, after all, was developed in the 1960s and 1970s by the US military, specifically by the Defense Advanced Research Projects Agency (DARPA) in conjunction with a few research universities, with the goal of being able to communicate effectively in the event of a nuclear war.[66] Thus, if one "node" on the network (say, Chicago) were destroyed by a thermonuclear device, then traffic would simply find another way, through other nodes, to continue moving and eventually reach its destination.

Once it was broadly available to universities in the 1980s and the general public in the 1990s, the Internet's decentralized structure was quickly heralded as inherently democratic because it didn't rely on hierarchies and control and didn't privilege one website or person over another. It was a medium where anyone who had access to the necessary technology and infrastructure could create and distribute "content." In fact, many people still talk about the Internet as a liberating medium that can spread democracy by creating unfettered access to information and ideas. Net neutrality is a key part of this vision. It means that the Internet doesn't treat some people's information differently from other people's; it doesn't take sides to slow down some communications and speed up others; it stays true to the democratic structure of the original Internet. Unfortunately—as with so much technology that begins with democratic potential—this ideal is quickly becoming obsolete. Internet service providers (ISPs) like Verizon and search engines like Google are teaming up to implement differentiated service throughout the Internet, so people or companies that can pay will have their data routed faster. A version of this has existed for a while with different service plans (dial-up, DSL, cable). But these speed and convenience controls just limit the transfer speeds that ISPs allow; they don't change the ways packets of information are treated. With the demise of net neutrality, however, this system of equal treatment is over: peer-to-peer computing networks can be slowed down while MSN.com is sped up; Google could slow down users' access to Amazon.com but speed up their access to YouTube (which it owns); the websites of activist groups could grind to a standstill while Fox News achieves blazing speeds. This process, already under way, could further undermine the democratic ideals of the Internet and fully transform it into a privatized medium where "the only services left on the public Internet would provide crappy, slow, and ad-laden content."[67]

Surveillance is an important part of the demise of net neutrality. The top ISPs and search engines actively monitor which activities generate profits for them and which ones threaten those profits. Peer-to-peer file sharing on sites like BitTorrent may lend itself to piracy (illegally downloading copyrighted movies, songs, or games without paying required fees), and this may threaten profits, which could be why the giant cable and media company Comcast has intentionally slowed down or blocked access to this service in the past.[68] Similarly, independent news media sites and blogs could be slowed down or censored because they challenge the dominant messages generated by mainstream media outlets, which happen to be owned by—or have close relationships with—service providers. In this vein, Google censors independent news from its Google News search engine, which requires careful monitoring and surveillance on its part.[69]

In sum, through surveillance, Internet users may be "socially sorted" and prioritized based on what they pay and what they do. But content providers from all points on the ideological spectrum may be slowed down and censored too. Another reason the neutrality of the Internet is so important to the politics of surveillance is that a great part of the surveillance society operates through the Internet. That's where the data are gathered, moved, and managed. As long as the Net stays free, the possibilities for access and challenge remain stronger. But it appears that the democratic potential of the Internet may be on the chopping block.

Deep in Your Packets

Many universities are now using servers to scan or preemptively block certain kinds of Internet traffic. Should you be downloading music, movies, or software from a peer-to-peer file-sharing service like BitTorrent or Kazaa, they will know. How? One increasingly popular technology is called "deep packet inspection" (DPI). In the old days, servers just looked at the header of any packet of information being sent over the Internet (the header is like an address on an envelope telling the network where the message should go and where it's been). With DPI, servers or firewalls can see the content of the packets, so if they know what a song or movie packet looks like, they can discover matches on the university network and block them in real time.[70] Next, if the files are illegal, they might come after you with disciplinary action or turn you over to the authorities for jail time or hefty fines—of about $22,500 per song![71]

Eyes on the Street

The past several years have seen a host of new technologies through which virtual and physical spaces converge, overlap, and create new opportunities for surveillance. Google Street View is a perfect example of this. The Google company has sent out platoons of vehicles equipped with 360-degree cameras, GPS units, and WiFi readers to drive through neighborhoods around the world and take continuous digital photographs of everything along the way: houses, cars, trees, vacant lots, people, and other animals. All these data are then made available through the Street View application, so that if you enter an address you can pull up an image of the location, see vehicles parked out front, see people picnicking on the lawn. In case you're wondering, the current Google policy is to blur faces or license plates, but a lot of information can be gleaned even without seeing faces. One woman was especially disturbed to find out that Street View could zoom all the way in to her second-story apartment window to show her cat sitting on a perch in the living room.[72] And the driver of a Google Street View vehicle was probably dismayed to learn that after he accidentally hit a fawn, Street View users found before-and-after images (cute deer in the road; dead deer on the pavement) and plastered them over the Internet asking, "Who killed Bambi?"[73]

In addition to visual photos, though, Street View sucks in as much information as possible—like tracking available WiFi networks and assessing whether they're password protected. This got Google into a lot of trouble when European regulators found out that between 2006 and 2010 Google had been collecting tons of personal information about individuals as its cars drove along residential streets.[74] In violation of privacy laws in Europe, if people didn't have their networks encrypted, Google's cars read the websites they viewed and even the content of their e-mail. Google was investigated by European regulators and fined for these infractions.[75] According to the German minister for food, agriculture, and consumer protection, these violations are further evidence that "privacy law is a foreign concept to Google."[76] This is probably not that much of an overstatement, given the way Google, Facebook, and other companies seem to view it as "fair game" to collect, store, analyze, and trade anything that can be converted into data, which nowadays is just about anything.

The Internet of Things

Your computer and cell phone aren't the only things connected to the Internet. A host of "smart" devices are slowly entering our homes, offices, and cars. We know some of them are beaming information across the Internet, such as TiVo and other entertainment technologies that download television schedules and silently report our viewing habits back to the media companies.[77] This is a kind of surveillance that allows media companies to compile profiles of users and sell those data to advertisers, just like the other web-based applications we've been talking about. But did you ever suspect that your washing machine, refrigerator, or air conditioner could be spying on you?

What's been called the Internet of Things describes this connecting of all electronic grids and appliances to the Internet so that each item has a unique number (an IP address) that can be accessed remotely. Once they have IP addresses and are connected to the Internet, they can "talk" to other devices or applications and be controlled from remote locations. Don't have WiFi in your home or business? That's not a huge problem. What's known as powerline Ethernet can allow you—or others—to use existing electrical lines to transfer information just like an Ethernet cable does. In fact, one of us currently uses a powerline Ethernet system in his home so he can achieve faster transfer speeds than a typical WiFi network. Don't have WiFi in your car? No problem there either, because cellular technology can talk to your car just fine, even when you're moving at high speeds. In one recent case, for instance, a disgruntled former employee of a used-car dealership in Texas logged into the dealership's website, disabled the ignition systems of more than a hundred cars that had been sold to customers, then set off all the cars' alarms.[78] This wireless pager-based system was supposed to allow the dealership to disable people's cars if they didn't pay their loans on time. The car owners were furious to wake up to honking horns and flashing lights on cars that wouldn't start!

The implications of the Internet of Things are huge. You could have a "smart" house or office building that turns on lights or heat only when someone is in the room; that alerts you that one office is losing more heat (or cool air) than others and might need new windows or insulation; that turns off all your gas appliances if your smoke detector goes off.[79] Smart-grid systems currently let electric companies monitor your energy consumption from a distance and turn off your power if you don't pay your bill or if they need to perform a rolling blackout to save electrical grids. Soon electric companies may be able to turn off your appliances or change your thermostat if they think you're using too much electricity during peak hours.

This isn't science fiction. During a record heat wave in the summer of 2010, the utility company in New York City sent radio signals to some twenty thousand air-conditioning thermostats, programming them to cycle off and on every thirty minutes, effectively raising building temperatures and removing control from residents and tenants.[80] At the moment such "load shedding" interventions are done to prevent blackouts and are often voluntary programs that customers join to get reduced rates.[81] But there's a fine line between incentive and coercion, because some people will be priced out of the "choice" of maintaining control. This will probably become another form of social sorting, where these particular surveillance systems will give better service to those who can afford to pay, while others will just have to sweat or freeze. And soon these voluntary programs will likely become mandatory, slowly implemented without most people being aware of it.

Conclusion

Almost everything we do online generates data that can be used for surveillance purposes, some we condone and some we don't, some we're aware of and many more we're not. It's also clear that all worlds are rapidly becoming interlinked with online ones, where sensors are embedded in mundane devices and most interactions are mediated in some way by electronic systems. In this world, surveillance is everywhere to the extent that information and communication technologies are everywhere. So it's incredibly difficult and often impractical and undesirable to avoid it.

One response from online companies like Facebook or Google is to lower people's expectations for privacy and control, to get them used to total exposure. For example, the CEO of Google, Eric Schmidt, says, "If you have something that you don't want anyone to know, maybe you shouldn't be doing it in the first place."[82] Such statements, if we accepted them, would let companies like Google off the hook. But it's obviously absurd to imply that users must be doing something wrong if there are things they don't want broadcast. For instance, do you want your medical records, stored in a personal health record system, shared? Do you want your online banking information shared? Do you want your visit to a gay bar shared? Do you want your IM courtship of a girlfriend or boyfriend shared with your parents, teachers, or employers? Do you want all your Google searches shared with the world? Pause and think about that one: What online searches would you prefer to keep secret?

Because online worlds so easily allow the collection, analysis, storage, and trading of data, they also make surveillance very easy. What seems to be happening is that online companies, government agencies, and other organizations have found these forms of surveillance too alluring and too profitable to ignore. To entice us to participate, we're offered convenience, social belonging, discounts, and a bunch of free apps. So we "opt in." But this story is too simplistic. It implies that the choices we're given are real choices, meaning that we can say, "No, thank you," without any repercussions.

This brings us back to the point we raised at the beginning of this chapter—a lot of online-based surveillance is voluntary, in a way. Sometimes we want people to see us, we want to share personal experiences with our friends, and we want to find our friends when we go out somewhere. Other times we'd prefer to reveal less information, but online applications can be so convenient that we willingly give in to get music or movie recommendations, search for things on the web, or read an electronic version of a newspaper or magazine story.

What happens is that (if we think about them at all) we accept these things as "choices"—trade-offs in which we give up personal information for convenience. But in reality there's little choice, because we can't truly opt out if we need to function in the contemporary world. Instead of choice, maybe *coercion* is a better way to think about our relation to online surveillance. After all, your university may force you to get a Gmail account, your employer may require constant access by e-mail or smartphone, utility companies may (soon) require that bills be paid electronically, and your social life may be toast if you don't use IM, text messaging, or Facebook. Are these really choices if the costs of saying no are so high?

We also think these are false trade-offs because *it is possible*, in reality, to have more convenience without giving up all your data to third-party advertisers and the like. Our ability to effectively navigate the web does not, in fact, require that one corporation amass troves of information about ourselves and our lives. We just take it for granted that the technologies have to be this way.

Sure, people can take some intriguing techno-precautions to manage their lives online. You could use proxy servers to anonymize your searches, you could encrypt your e-mails and force recipients to use cryptographic keys to read them, and you could delete your browser's cookies after every session. Some of these responses are too technical for basic users; some reduce the performance of your equipment; and some, like deleting or not accepting cookies, will make browsing less convenient by forcing you to log in to websites and reenter information manually every time.

Probably a better long-term response would be to raise expectations for the protection of personal data, to regulate online surveillance so people are automatically opted out of information sharing rather than automatically opted in, and to penalize companies that violate users' trust. This response would demand that we recognize the importance of keeping information in the contexts where it was generated: Facebook postings shouldn't be shared with employers, Google searches shouldn't be shared with anyone, Google Street View shouldn't collect information about people's WiFi networks, and so forth. From an American perspective, this may seem unimaginable, but it's obvious and basic to people in many other countries. Germany, for instance, has regulations preventing employers from consulting Facebook when making hiring decisions,[83] and the Czech Republic suspended Google Street View over concerns about privacy protections.[84] If companies are told that the law requires them to collect and share less information and to protect data better, they'll figure out a way to comply, just as they do in other countries.

At the very least, we hope more people will question the discursive framing of these issues. Do we really have much control? No. Does it imply that we're doing something wrong if we'd like to keep things hidden? No. Is opting in to online surveillance a choice, or is it coercion? It's both.

4: Surveillance in Schools

- When the high schools in the Philadelphia suburb of Lower Merion, Pennsylvania, gave their students free laptops, the principals didn't brag about one special app—a program that could secretly take pictures with the laptops' cameras. School staff could also capture screen content, monitor texting, and identify the location of online computers. More than fifty thousand pictures of family rooms, bedrooms, and half-dressed students had been captured and stored on the schools' computer systems. The surveillance capacity had been installed so the schools could trace lost or stolen computers, but soon text messages were being monitored for signs of conflict, and bedroom photos were scrutinized to see if a student was eating candy or taking prescription medicine.[1]
- When Savana Redding was an eighth-grade honors student at Arizona's Safford Middle School, a classmate claimed the thirteen-year-old had prescription-strength ibuprofen (equivalent to two Advil tablets), in violation of her school's zero-tolerance antidrug policy. Savana said she didn't. Soon she was in the school office, weeping, as she was stripped to her underwear and searched. Then she was ordered to shake out her bra and panties. There were no pills. Savana's mother worked with the American Civil Liberties Union to take the case all the way to the Supreme Court, where a rare agreement of all the justices except Clarence Thomas found that the school authorities had violated the girl's rights.[2]
- In May 1996 the students of Alexander High School in rural southeastern Ohio were startled to see the school invaded by black-hooded police officers with drug-sniffing dogs. The principal of the small high school had called in the local narcotics squad. Students

and teachers were held in lockdown in their classrooms until the agents left, having found no illegal drugs at all.[3]

- Each year, millions of standardized assessment tests survey almost every student in America to see if mandated state and federal proficiency levels are being achieved. Many schools devote weeks or months to preparing for the tests and have redesigned their entire educational mission to align with the profile of the exams. In some schools, students who pass the tests get special rewards or release time. In others, students who might not pass are urged to drop out or stay home on test days so they don't make the school look bad.[4]

If you've been to a school recently, you know that secret spy cams, strip searches, drug sweeps, and tests are just a few examples among the many old and new surveillance practices used in the education industry. In fact, schools are so completely defined by surveillance that sometimes it's hard to even recognize it for what it is. But if we recall that a basic definition of surveillance is using observation and information to manage people, it's pretty obvious that Central High School could just as well be called Surveillance Central.

School surveillance begins with the earliest moments of registration, when parents enroll their children in the local school system. (For some high-demand preschools and kindergartens, parents register them before they're born!) Then medical exams and vaccinations are verified. Next comes the whole blur of activities that you vaguely remember—daily attendance, annual attendance reports, hall passes, quizzes, tests, notes about sick days, grades, achievement and proficiency exams. These are all part of the everyday routine for most students, and they are *all* mechanisms of surveillance used to manage a population. In fact, we could write a whole book just on the subject of school surveillance (and it has been done).[5]

Schools are one of the key social settings where innovations in surveillance technology are first deployed. In a pattern similar to what we see in prisons and the military, the availability of large numbers of semi-citizens under daily institutional control has made schools leading laboratories for new surveillance practices. There are closed-circuit television (CCTV) cameras, metal detectors, radio-frequency identification (RFID) cards, RFID-embedded uniforms, fingerprint readers, locker searches, transparent book bags, pat-downs, drug-sniffing dogs, drug tests, and much more. It isn't just teachers and administrators who watch students, either. On-site police officers and security guards investigate infractions; military recruiters amass dossiers on potential recruits and pressure them to enlist; and private companies collect marketing data through "educational" software and websites.[6] Almost everything about schools is oriented toward making students visible and controllable.

This chapter looks at some of the latest developments in school surveillance and questions their effects. We start from the position that, just like everyone else, students are learning all the time, from every interaction and every event. It's not just the official curriculum or planned classroom activities that teach them. Interactions with others teach students whether they are important, whether their opinions count, whether they are empowered, whether they are dangerous (or in danger), whether people care about them, or whether formal education is worthwhile. Additionally, styles of testing and assessment carry implicit lessons about the world—that there are always right and wrong answers or that "knowledge" can be measured in objective ways. So as we describe elements of school surveillance, we'll be focusing on these many hidden lessons.

The School Security Movement

School security is big business, with sales teams poised to combine scare tactics, reassurance, and razzle-dazzle with technology and promises of efficiency. But a lot of it comes down to maintaining a high level of fear. The website for RaptorWare, for example, features a news update window with the latest examples of sexual predators gaining access to school grounds[7] and then makes the following pitch:

RaptorWare: Do You Know, Really Know, Who Is Coming in and out of Your Facility?

Thousands of schools and community facilities across the country use Raptor's V-soft visitor management and screening technology to help protect children from sex offenders, domestic dispute offenders and other trespassers. V-soft works in conjunction with law enforcement to add an extra layer of security and keep our kids safe.[8]

Another firm, Garrett Metal Detectors, offers a range of systems for detecting weapons in schools, at airports, and in prisons. Their product line includes a "tactical" handheld scanner that sends a silent vibration to the user so people being scanned don't know if they're triggering an alert—this will give the user "continual tactical advantage" over the (potentially dangerous) subjects being scanned.[9] The company's sales pitch mixes fear with pragmatics:

In recent years America has experienced an unprecedented number of deadly shootings on school campuses. . . . Minor schoolyard scuffles have evolved into major violent incidents, with guns replacing fists as the weapons of choice. . . . Ensuring the safety of students and staff is an ongoing challenge facing many educational institutions across our nation. However, thanks in part to metal detection technology, it is a challenge that is being met.[10]

According to such companies, the only responsible course is for schools to buy their equipment and implement full-scale security plans.

Whether the threat is from outside, in the form of predators, or inside, in the form of students with weapons or drugs, the purveyors of surveillance technologies promise to help school administrators secure their worlds. These companies, and many more, have been part of a movement in which schools have dramatically expanded the reach of their surveillance systems.

Given all you've likely read and seen about the dangers that await America's schoolchildren, it may surprise you to hear that kids are much safer at school than at home. There's a *one in 3.2 million chance* that a student might suffer a homicide or suicide at school; that's roughly equivalent to seventeen a year.[11] But a reported 1,530 children die outside school each year from abuse or neglect.[12] The truth is that schools are some of *the* safest places for kids—much safer than riding in a car, playing in the neighborhood, or staying home.[13]

But dispassionate public policy data are typically unable to stand up against the rare but truly frightening instances of serious violence in schools. The horrifying tragedy of the 1999 shootings at Columbine High School in Colorado—where two students killed thirteen victims before committing suicide—appalled the world and became a symbol of violence in schools.[14] Public officials called for stricter gun control laws and bold new measures for school surveillance. The latter proposals saw more success. Oddly, even though Columbine had advanced surveillance—a comprehensive video-monitoring system and an armed security guard—it still became a rallying cry for schools to spend more money on people and machinery designed to watch and control students. Soon large amounts of federal money were available to upgrade school security systems, and school districts lined up to apply for grants.

After 9/11, even more federal money was made available for school security systems. It was suggested that schools might be the next target for terrorist attacks, so the Department of Homeland Security created a matching grant program to subsidize surveillance systems and coordination with local police.[15] Shortly thereafter, schools across the country, regardless of size or budget, were installing the latest gear, writing emergency evacuation plans, and running emergency drills with police and other first responders.[16] As a result, 77 percent of US schools were using video surveillance by 2008.[17] All this is in addition to metal detectors, identification cards, on-site security personnel, and other protective measures.

Camera Creeps

It's a bad idea to have cameras installed in a school locker room. At one public middle school in Livingston, Tennessee, school administrators repeatedly watched digital recordings of students undressing. Most of the victims were ten- to fourteen-year-old girls.[18] According to Internet service provider records, administrators accessed the recordings ninety-eight times, at all hours of the night, and from several states.[19]

No Need to Call the Cops

Now, in many schools, closed-circuit television cameras and armed police officers monitor the hallways, metal detectors check for weapons, drug dogs sniff lockers and backpacks, and drug-testing programs test students' urine for evidence of illegal drug use. In others it's a bit more low-key—principals roam the halls and survey the lunchrooms, guidance counselors reach out to at-risk students, ID cards monitor and control access, special programs identify problems and intervene when things start to go wrong. As a rule, poorer schools with more minority students experience the first hard-core forms of surveillance and control, while whiter, more affluent schools go for the subtler approaches.[20] With zero-tolerance policies for drugs and weapons and a stronger police presence in lower-income schools, we're also seeing a rising use of criminal sanctions for school-based misconduct, especially when it's minority youth who are misbehaving.[21]

Whereas students once might have received a detention or suspension for fighting in school, for example, today many students are charged with assault for the same behavior, courtesy of on-site school resource officers (SROs), who are police officers assigned to schools.[22] The ability to amass a criminal record for minor infractions has contributed to what scholars call the school-to-prison pipeline, especially for inner-city, minority males.[23] This trend clearly contributes to the incarceration epidemic in the United States, which now keeps close to 2.3 million people behind bars.[24] African American males in particular bear the brunt of this, since they are incarcerated seven times as often as whites.[25]

Currently SROs walk the hallways of 68 percent of all high schools and middle schools in the United States.[26] There's no need to call the cops if something goes wrong, because they're already there. These police officers, along with security guards, do much more than simply respond to crimes at schools, though. In their attempts to deter crime or investigate nonschool crimes, they engage in systematic surveillance that dramatically alters the school environment. For instance, many SROs see themselves as role models, so they eagerly chat with students, offer career advice, and encourage confidences. At the same time, SROs are cultivating "informants" who can tell them about parties, burglaries, or drug deals so the police can intervene. Similarly, when students are questioned about wrongdoing or searched for illegal items, SROs are frequently in the room with administrators and sometimes lead the interrogations themselves.[27] This is a big problem, because it circumvents constitutional rights. Students are questioned without being read their Miranda rights; they are searched without probable cause; and they can be formally charged for any crime discovered.[28]

For all you "tough on crime" readers out there, we should point out that a lot of students are being punished for ridiculous things. Six-year-old Zachary Christie was suspended for bringing his new Cub Scout fork-spoon-knife tool to his first-grade class to show his friends.[29] Some students have been arrested for smuggling their cell phones onto school grounds, and others have been arrested for stepping out of a metal-detector line.[30] And how about doing time for a food fight? In 2009, twenty-five students at Calumet Middle School in Chicago were arrested, hauled off to jail, and charged with the misdemeanor of "reckless conduct" for participating in a glorious food fight.[31] Like a chemistry experiment, when you combine zero-tolerance policies, fear, surveillance, and the police, these are some of the unexpected reactions that are produced.

Are You Allowed to Eat That?

The ongoing erosion of trust at schools can take many forms. For instance, hundreds of schools have now implemented biometric fingerprinting to monitor and regulate student access to cafeteria food. The way the systems work is fairly straightforward: students have their fingerprints "captured" by an optical reader; the fingerprint is converted into numerical code and associated with the student's name or identification number; then whenever the student wants to buy a lunch, she has to scan her fingerprint to make sure she's permitted to eat.[32] Some systems let parents prepay for food online through a website interface.[33] Students who qualify for federally subsidized meals are scanned the same way, but the bill goes to Uncle Sam.[34] In the eyes of many parents and school administrators, the fingerprint system is much better than cash, because students might lose money—or give it away, or use it on other things.[35] So far so good, but the surveillance functions are robust.

With these biometric systems, student purchases can be tracked, analyzed, and controlled. As one story describes it, the system "allows parents to pre-pay for school lunches as well as monitor their children's food choices. The technology even enables parents to restrict their children's choices to avoid 'special diet' conflicts or to prevent children from purchasing high fat, high sugar a la carte items."[36] If a student tries to buy a slice of pizza or a soda but his parents have ruled out those options, the purchases will be denied. How embarrassing! Parents will also know exactly what their children bought (and presumably ate), so they can talk to them about it later (or punish them). This becomes one more way parents can remotely monitor their kids at school, similar to online dashboards that let them view report cards or test results.[37]

And whereas sometimes function creep is accidental and unanticipated, with student biometric systems it is *planned*. For instance, the system at one elementary school "can be expanded, at no additional cost, to handle time and attendance, event admission, parking lot security and the tracking of students riding on school buses."[38] At other schools the systems can be tapped to check out library books.[39] And a similar "palm reading" system in Scotland allows school officials "to provide biometric access control, monitor truancy levels, keep an eye on class attendance, and provide time management [i.e., workplace surveillance] of staff."[40] With an integrated biometric system, just about any student or staff activity can be monitored and stored in digital records.

Regardless of the intended purpose, the message for students is to cooperate with this extended control and get used to it. In academic language, we would say that students are "normalized" to this surveillance—it becomes commonplace, unquestioned, and unremarkable. When biometric systems were first introduced in the 2000s, some parents and civil liberties groups protested, and a few schools decided to nix the systems.[41] Nowadays there's no debate and almost no news coverage; instead, parents simply fill out forms so their children can be fingerprinted and entered into the database.

There's a lot of pressure on parents to comply, too. When all the other kids in the school scan their fingers to eat lunch, how stigmatizing would it be for your child to need a special system? In some cases, when parents have refused because of privacy concerns, they've been told their children wouldn't be allowed to eat school lunches at all.[42] Opted-out children have been *forced* to give fingerprint scans, too.[43] In a climate of complete, expected cooperation, there's little room for autonomy, either for students or for parents. The "lessons" for students are that they aren't trusted with cash or food choices, that they should accept daily fingerprinting without question, and that deviation from the norm will be punished.

Tracking Kids Like Cattle

Taking attendance at large public schools can be difficult. When some high schools have over four thousand students,[44] recording attendance is a major paperwork burden for teachers and absorbs precious time that could be spent on lessons, testing, or other things. But because public schools receive revenue based on the number of students on campus, school administrators have a financial incentive to count everyone present. But many times students come to school, enter the fenced-in facility, but don't actually go to every class; instead they roam the hallways, socialize in the gym, and play cat-and-mouse with security personnel charged with rounding them up.[45] And skipping class may not really matter in the grand scheme of things—school authorities just need to count the students somehow in order to get public funding.[46]

The solution? Radio-frequency identification badges. These badges can track class attendance too, but students don't have to go to class to get counted. They're scanned as they pass through the front gates and logged as "present" at school. By installing these systems, some school districts claim they've been able to recoup about $100,000 a year in state funding they would otherwise have lost.[47]

But saving money can seem like a crude reason for exposing kids to high-tech surveillance, so school districts have woven a bunch of scary yarns about child abductors, students trapped in burning buildings, and other security and safety threats supposedly countered by their RFID systems.[48] While these fanciful threat and rescue scenarios might be theoretically possible, none have been demonstrated, and many parents and students see right through the rhetoric. Parents have complained about students' being used as guinea pigs in technological experiments,[49] and commentators have drawn comparisons with tracking livestock: "RFID might be fine for monitoring inventory in a warehouse or cattle on the range, but it is inexcusable to treat students like a side of beef."[50]

Nonetheless, school districts from the United States to Japan are rolling out these systems and requiring students to use them. The Texas Education Agency, for example, has said that while schools shouldn't force students to carry RFID badges, they can "take disciplinary action" if they don't.[51] So much for choice. The coverage of the systems is increasing, too. Some schools have placed RFID detectors on buses, in hallways, in cafeterias, and over bathroom doors so students' whereabouts can be tracked at all times.[52] Students definitely notice the surveillance. One Texas sixth-grader confided, "It feels like someone's watching you at all times."[53] A classmate of hers elaborated, "It makes you mindful knowing you could get caught if you do something wrong."[54] Just like Michel Foucault wrote about the panopticon, when kids feel someone *might* be watching all the time, they may discipline themselves just in case.

Then again, RFID systems are notoriously insecure, which could invite mischievous kids—or ill-intentioned adults—to mess with the chips. With relatively cheap handheld "skimmers," people have successfully read RFID cards from thirty feet away.[55] You could probably write a cell phone app to do it. Once a card is skimmed, it's not hard to program a new card with the captured information.[56] We can imagine all kinds of scenarios where tech-savvy kids steal each other's RFID numbers, circulate multiple copies of cards, or otherwise appropriate the system. We'd have done that in a heartbeat back in high school.

The lessons from these RFID surveillance systems are a bit subtler than simply creating new vulnerabilities for students. As the quotations show, the systems communicate that students should behave for fear of getting caught, not because it's the right thing to do. Also, the systems care more about being on school grounds than being in the classroom, which could send the message that containment and counting are more important than education. Finally, just as with the cafeteria fingerprinting systems, opting out is not a viable option, so clear value is placed on conformity, not individuality.

The Blackboard Universe

The software platform known as Blackboard has swept the education industry. Teachers use it to communicate with classes, organize assigned readings, and host online discussions. But did you know about all the nifty surveillance features Blackboard brings to a teacher's desktop? Traditional services like recording attendance, managing a grade book, and keeping notes on students' performance are all there. But Blackboard also lets instructors monitor exactly which students open up which online readings and when they do it. Blackboard also counts up the frequency and length of online postings to discussion boards. Through Blackboard's paper-submission portal, students' writings are compared with writings across the Internet and with all papers that have ever been submitted through Blackboard's SafeAssign portal. Not surprisingly, if a school wants to branch out, Blackboard also provides campuses with comprehensive video surveillance installations.[57]

Testing

If you've ever been a student, you've almost certainly taken a test. In fact, you've probably got a career's worth of tests. You may not have thought of them as one small part of learning to live in the surveillance society, but that's what they are. It started very early with diagnostic testing in preschool or kindergarten, progressed to simple arithmetic and reading tests, then escalated to pulse-pounding midterms and anxiety-inducing *finals*. We devote a lot of energy to assessing students' learning. Papers, exams, and quizzes are long-standing icons of stress, fear, and accomplishment. In the past few decades, machine-gradable exams and computerized testing have emerged as relatively low-cost ways of assessing large numbers of students and bypassing the idiosyncrasies and discretion of classroom teachers. The educational system has adapted to this new surveillance technology with remarkable speed.

Now kindergartners do special assignments teaching them how to use their number 2 pencils to fill in the oval bubble below the little duckie or the pretty pony. Later they use this valuable skill to take state and federally mandated tests and college entrance exams like the ACT and the SAT. Even later, they can sign up for the GRE, the GMAT, or the LSAT (there's no end to the places you'll go with the right bubble-filling skills).

In fact, there's so much testing that the nation faces a shortage of qualified test writers. The critical job of designing test questions is being shopped out to freelancers who respond to ads saying things like, "Here's an opportunity to get paid by writing test questions for high-school students. . . . Just think of it . . . instead of you taking the test, you're actually the one making the questions!! That's something nice for a change!"[58]

No Child Left Behind

No Child Left Behind (NCLB) was a sweeping 2002 law designed to implement a national system of educational accountability by regularly testing US students to see if they meet state-designed standards for educational attainment. Under the law, kids are tested each year from grades three through eight, then once more in high school. NCLB means it's not just students who are graded by the tests, but teachers and whole schools as well. According to the guidelines, a school's scores on statewide tests must demonstrate adequate academic progress for the student body as a whole as well as major subgroups within it. Subgroups typically include the learning disabled, the poor, those with limited English, and all major racial and ethnic groups. If a school or any subgroup fails to show adequate performance, consequences range from shaming in published reports to closing a school and firing the staff. In some states performance bonuses and raises are tied to test results. Just imagine how seriously teachers and principals feel about tests when their livelihoods depend on it.

When important consequences are attached to tests (that's why they're called *high-stakes*), people naturally adjust their behavior. College-bound students flock to courses and programs that promise high scores, and teachers reorganize their days to make sure testing drills get plenty of time. We've also seen a shift in style of instruction as schools move away from things that don't directly contribute to teaching the skills needed to do well on the tests. Many of you have lived through the changes: cutbacks in art, music, gym, and other subjects not covered on the tests are accompanied by "back to basics" approaches to math, science, and reading, which are covered. Some schools take the added steps of pretest pep rallies, bonus days off for students who pass, and special prep courses for those who struggle. Just as students adapt the way they study to their knowledge of the teacher and the upcoming test, teachers tailor their teaching to the content of the statewide tests. Obviously, then, the tests do more than just watch. They re-create a nation's classrooms.

This observation is an important lesson about the broader politics of the surveillance society. While the direct translation of surveillance may be "watching from above," surveillance is not, of course, just about watching. It's watching with a purpose. Frequently the purpose is modifying behavior. Closed-circuit television cameras are not installed just so a security officer can enjoy stirring video coverage of a parking garage. They're there to observe *and* discourage unwanted activity. Drug tests aren't just a disinterested study of the personal lives of students, truck drivers, and job applicants. They're administered with the goal of detecting *and* discouraging illegal drug use. And tests aren't just about seeing how much you know about long division. They're about conditioning you and teachers to perform in certain ways and accept being evaluated on your performance.

Additionally, with new testing regimes, we get a standardizing of content over thousands of classrooms, schools, and districts; a centralized command to focus on measurable basics like readin' and writin' and 'rithmetic; and a displacement of local authority by state and national test-makers. With this, the powers of surveillance may well have achieved a fundamental reorganization of the practices of local control in American public education. In this light, large-scale surveillance can be understood as a powerful mechanism for remaking the world.

The Volvo Effect

The Volvo effect is a famous concept in the world of those who spend a lot of time thinking about standardized testing.[59] It's probably a bit out-of-date and should now be called the Lexus effect or the Mercedes effect. It comes from the simple fact that family income is a powerful predictor of performance on standardized tests—in short, count up the number of upscale vehicles in a driveway or neighborhood, and you can get a pretty good sense of how the kids will score on their tests. In fact, a number of studies have found that much of the variation in test scores can be explained by differences in wealth, income, and family status.[60] Why? Lots of reasons. Some argue that it's tied to the cultural biases built into the tests and how they relate to the lives of the tested. (Essay questions about shopping malls make a lot more sense to kids who spend time in malls.) Another likely reason is that more affluent families have the time and money for test preparation books or even dedicated classes or tutoring sessions. More affluent families can also send their kids to the test center with a healthful breakfast and a top-notch calculator. Also, since affluence and educational achievement are closely linked in most—if not all—societies, more affluent families may simply take testing more seriously. Finally, since the income of many school districts comes primarily from property taxes, spending on schools usually reflects the wealth of the community. The class bias here is obvious. But don't overlook the implications for the long struggle with racial discrimination—given the close ties between race and affluence, standardized tests mask long-standing patterns of discrimination under a cloak of scientific meritocracy.

Resistance and Opposition at Schools

It's fascinating that people almost always find ways to resist or oppose surveillance. Even with something as vast and daunting as standardized testing, there's always some sort of negotiation as people probe the boundaries of control relationships, try to get away with things, or fight for their rights. Resistance can sometimes undermine surveillance efforts, but its true power is in dispelling myths of neutrality and objectivity and revealing how institutional forms of control are always political and often discriminatory.

Standardized tests have been amazingly productive at generating creative forms of resistance and cheating. And we're not talking just about cheating by students, which is old news. Across the United States, teachers, principals, and other school employees have engaged in systematic cheating by coaching students, telling them the answers, leaving helpful information on chalkboards, or correcting students' tests after the fact. It's not just a few bad apples, either—it's systemic. In Atlanta, for instance, about two hundred administrators and teachers did this in forty-four out of fifty-six schools. A subsequent investigation found that "the cheating was organized, that educators and administrators would wear gloves so their fingerprints wouldn't be detected and held cheating parties where they'd get together and change grades."[61]

At a school in Washington, DC, students' scores improved so dramatically that each teacher received two bonuses of $8,000, and the principal was awarded two bonuses of $10,000.[62] Upon auditing, the testing company found a statistically improbable rate of "wrong-to-right" erasures of test answers for that school and over a hundred other schools in the city. In fact, according to statisticians, "the odds are better for winning the Powerball grand prize than having that many erasures by chance."[63] Oops, busted! (By a secondary surveillance inspection, no less.)

Just as you, or someone you know, may have been tempted to cheat on a test, teachers and administrators are falling prey to the same temptations. There are many motivations for it. In some areas, teachers' salaries and bonuses are tied to students' scores, so it's a matter of money. In other areas, test scores from a teacher's classroom are posted in the media, so it's a matter of pride. In other situations, it's a fight against a testing system that teachers see as unnecessary, discriminatory, and insulting. For others, it's to protect a school from NCLB sanctions that might leave children even worse off. In some cases, it seems teachers just can't stop teaching: they naturally want to help their students with a tough problem. The reasons often overlap, but they all point to an ongoing struggle against a surveillance system seen as unfair and unjust.

Colorful forms of resistance to school surveillance have cropped up in other arenas as well. In 2005, DeWitt Clinton High School in New York City started forcing all students to go through metal detectors to ensure compliance with a policy against cell phones, iPods, or other prohibited items on campus. Students perceived this as patently unfair and possibly discriminatory, especially since a more affluent public school a few blocks away was not imposing similar restrictions. The school told students they should arrive early to allow time for the screening, which required them to remove belts, jewelry, and boots, much like systems at airports. They would not be granted any leeway if they were late because of waiting in lines. And to top it off, all off-campus lunch privileges were revoked in favor of a new "captive lunch" program.[64]

What did students do? Roughly 1,500 of them held a walkout on the first day the new system went into effect.[65] Instead of just leaving campus, they trooped to the superintendent's office, accompanied by media and police, where they demanded a meeting and insisted on change. After the dust settled, the new protocol remained in place, but the walkout scored a huge symbolic victory and inspired other creative outlets, such as a student hip-hop group addressing inequality.[66]

On an everyday level, students play the system in a variety of ways. When they wander the hallways, even if they have hall passes, students tend to skirt police and security guards. They engage in counter-surveillance: watching the watchers, learning their patterns, and exercising evasion tactics to avoid being hassled.[67] Some female students intentionally flirt and cultivate rapport with security guards to increase their mobility (to go to the library, the bathroom, or leave campus and return without a note).[68] Still other students tempt fate by visiting pornographic websites on school computers, playing proscribed computer games, or misbehaving out of the sight of cameras or authority figures.[69] Such risk taking allows students to test the effectiveness of surveillance systems and improvise when they get caught; in these ways, they both assert agency and resist conformity.

Since surveillance systems are designed to manage us, it only makes sense that we do what we can to manage them. To those of us who study surveillance as a key part of the organization of power and control in society, questions of when, how, and why people cooperate with surveillance become very important. Cheating, school walkouts, avoiding or flirting with security guards, and risk taking are all symbolic challenges to the system. Perhaps with the exception of the school walkout, which started as a spontaneous event but quickly became organized, these measures are all tactics of *everyday resistance*—informal, unorganized, sometimes illegal means of thwarting a surveillance mechanism. Resistance is different from straight-out opposition, which covers things like public protests, litigation, and political organizing. Resistance is often quiet, even secret. It's unorganized. And it's usually explained in terms of personal interest or concern rather than grand claims to liberty, equality, or justice (though history suggests that almost anyone can make these arguments when pressed).

The Politics of Resistance

When we write about the political and social importance of everyday resistance, we're not necessarily arguing for its moral propriety. An observation that something is politics is not necessarily a claim that it's *good* politics. Whether or not something is good politics comes down to our personal assessment of right and wrong and who we'd like to see win in one of life's many skirmishes over power and resources.

Resistance defines all social systems, including schools but extending well beyond them. All sorts of things are covered under the idea of everyday resistance, and you've almost certainly done some of them. Working under the table; adjusting your time sheets; driving with a radar detector; using fake IDs; engaging in cash-and-barter economies; supplying clean urine; and cheating on tests are just a few of the many ways people find to evade, sidestep, or push back against surveillance. Few of these actions are socially important in their own right, but when we reimagine them as an international pattern in which millions of people find small ways to push back against the powers that govern their lives, everyday resistance takes on a critical new position in our exploration of life in the surveillance society.

Conclusion

There's something ironic about school surveillance. Education is the one institution most people associate with empowerment. This can be seen in ever-popular narratives of education offering a bridge to future employment and success, or leading to personal growth and fulfillment. The lessons taught by school surveillance, however, are inherently disempowering. Students are expected to obediently submit to metal detectors, searches, RFID tracking, fingerprinting, tests, and everything else. Through these surveillance rituals, they're taught that if they deviate from the norm or fail to follow rules, they'll be punished. Thanks to zero-tolerance policies for infractions, good excuses, misunderstandings, or remorse for wrongdoing may not matter at all. And the punishments can be harsh, such as being arrested by on-site police officers and racking up a criminal record without even leaving the school grounds.

It's no coincidence that Foucault included schools in his list of modern organizations that had disciplinary effects similar to the panopticon's.[70] Regimentation, order, visibility, and compliance are fundamental goals of educational institutions. Regardless of the official curriculum taught in classrooms or found in books, surveillance technologies and techniques infuse schools and shape students' experiences and development. Even the design of most schools prioritizes visibility, standardization, and control: Why else are desks lined up in neat rows with the teacher's desk in front?

Surveillance in schools is particularly insidious because it can be so hard to recognize. It's just how things are done! And when there are more obvious forms of surveillance, such as CCTV cameras or metal detectors, people tend to think of them as achieving discrete goals (e.g., student safety) without questioning their secondary, unanticipated effects. Some of the unplanned lessons of school surveillance are that school authorities and students can't trust one another, students have few rights, and rules are inflexible. Another lesson is that authority figures—from teachers to parents to police—force identities on students (threatening troublemaker or vulnerable victim) and deter them from developing alternative identities. Resistance to surveillance shows that there is still room for educational empowerment, but it may happen in spite of, rather than because of, the way schools are run.

5: Watching You Work

It was the moment Anna had been dreading. Ever since a coworker logged in to Anna's computer and sent the boss an e-mail saying, "I'm now in the office," she'd known it might come back to bite her. And it did. Here she was, standing in front of him, tears welling, trying to explain that she didn't tell her coworker to lie about what time she arrived. The boss didn't care, and he certainly didn't believe her. After all, his computer system had discovered the "fact" of the erroneous e-mail, and he was pleased with himself for unearthing a contradiction in Anna's record.

Because she typically got to the office at 6:00 a.m., well before any of the managers, Anna was supposed to send the boss an e-mail, and its time stamp would serve as a clock-in time. Her coworker *thought* she was doing her a favor by clocking her in when she was late for work. But the boss was suspicious—and maybe had way too much time on his hands. So he logged in to the electronic system for the building's parking garage, pulled up the time she swiped her parking card, and compared that with the time posted on the e-mail. Discrepancy discovered! The e-mail was sent forty-five minutes before Anna's car entered the garage.

With disbelief and anger mounting inside her, she listened to the gloating manager inform her that she was formally on probation and had better start looking for another job. It didn't matter that she routinely worked overtime without extra pay. It didn't matter that she never took the ten-minute breaks allowed by law. It didn't matter that she never tried to deceive anyone about what time she arrived. The electronic systems of the office and building had been transformed into surveillance systems, and the boss was eager to use them to punish her.

This story is not made up. It happened to one of our friends a few years back. And it's also not exceptional. Workplace surveillance is the norm for just about all jobs. Sometimes surveillance technologies are direct programs of observation clearly designed to monitor and discipline employees, like drug testing or keystroke tracking. Other times, as in Anna's story, the technologies are designed for different purposes (sending e-mail or entering a parking garage), but they lend themselves to surveillance. This second set of uses is what we've referred to in previous chapters as function creep, because the systems creep beyond their original purposes. Whatever you want to call it, the workplace is crawling with surveillance, and a lot of times people don't even realize it.

Taylorism: The Science of Working Faster

Workplaces have always been places of surveillance. In some accounts of early capitalism, one of the main reasons decentralized production systems were first implemented in shops and then in factories was so bosses could keep a closer eye on their workers. Whether people work in shops or offices, factories or fields, techniques of monitoring and control have been interwoven with labor processes for a long time. But workplace monitoring encountered a fundamental shift in the early twentieth century when a new idea was born: use "scientific" techniques to manage workers in factories to achieve optimal efficiency.

Frederick Winslow Taylor, one of the engineers at the heart of this new enterprise, used a stopwatch to time workers and analyzed their movements in an effort to discover the quickest and most efficient ways to perform repetitive tasks.[1] One of the problems he sought to eliminate was "soldiering," where workers would deliberately slow down to make labor less taxing and more tolerable. Taylor's method consisted of breaking down tasks into their components, assigning workers to the tasks they performed best, and disciplining those who did not consistently operate as quickly as possible.[2] This general technique was called scientific management; today it's often referred to as Taylorism.

Taylor was not simply looking to increase productivity and punish workers. He was advocating for the formation of a new managerial class that he thought could bring about social and economic prosperity by applying scientific principles to the workplace. In 1911 he wrote,

All the planning which under the old system was done by the workman, as a result of his personal experience, must of necessity under the new system be done by the management in accordance with the laws of the science. . . . One type of man is needed to plan ahead and an entirely different type to execute the work.[3]

From this quotation we see that Taylor was attempting to use scientific explanations to justify the subordination of workers and the elevation of managers and engineers. Even today we may perceive managers, who oversee our work, as a natural and necessary component of any organization, but it was men like Taylor who created this "necessity."[4]

One serious downside to scientific management is that it's dehumanizing—it treats workers like machine parts that can be manipulated and discarded at will. In 1913 some workers at a military arsenal wrote to their congressman:

We object to the use of the Stop Watch, as it is used [as] a means of speeding men up to a point beyond their normal capacity. It is humiliating and savors too much of the slave driver. . . . [The Stop Watch system] has resulted in accidents, inferior work and numerous abuses such as no American Citizen should be called upon to endure.[5]

In response to opposition by arsenal workers and trade unions, Congress eventually eliminated scientific management programs at all federal installations,[6] but the ideas have continued to shape management practices throughout many organizations.

Ford Had a Better Idea

Taylor wasn't the only one trying to get more out of workers. Drawing inspiration from the Chicago meatpacking industry, Henry Ford is often credited with instituting a version of scientific management in his automobile assembly lines. Ford's assembly lines are among the most famous icons of industrial efficiency—they allowed for important changes in the visibility and accountability of workers, who were now in the open, each performing one specialized task, under specific guidelines for speed and quality. But Ford's surveillance extended beyond the factory walls and into workers' homes. In 1913 Ford created a

Sociological Department (later renamed the Educational Department) to engage in a moral mission of monitoring workers outside the workplace to ensure that they were upright individuals of good character. The investigators of the Sociological Department "visited workers' homes gathering information and giving advice on the intimate details of the family budget, diet, living arrangements, recreation, social outlook, and morality."[7] Workers were put on probation or fired if they "refused to learn English, rejected the advice of the investigator, gambled, [or] drank excessively."[8]

While some of this may sound outrageously paternalistic today, employers still make judgments about employees' character based on how they look, how they talk, their sexual orientation, or whether they use prohibited recreational substances. Though many forms of discrimination are now illegal, that doesn't stop these practices from happening behind the scenes. And in some cases, as with drug testing, employees are still held accountable for what they do when they're not working, regardless of whether it affects their job performance. (More on this later.)

Surveillance in the Modern Workplace

Taylorism is alive and well in the surveillance society. The electronic systems we use at work automatically log almost everything we do, rendering our activities more "manageable" through analysis and comparison. In other words, workplace technologies simultaneously enable us to do our jobs *and* create data so others can evaluate our performance. Communications scholar Mark Andrejevic explains:

Keystroke monitoring programs, for example, deter employees from using computers for non-work-related activities while they simultaneously provide a detailed record of worker productivity. Bar code scanners in supermarkets serve not only to record prices, making the checkout worker's job faster and easier; they can also keep track of the checker's scan rate to monitor productivity, as can portable, networked, GPS-equipped devices for delivery workers and truckers.[9]

Even the American farmer, a long-standing icon of independence, might be driving a tractor with a GPS-computer interface that uses satellites to guide the plowing and provides full reports and maps on the day's coverage.[10] We've left the stopwatch in the dust. Taylor would be proud.

Currently about 75 percent of employees at American companies are subjected to *regular* surveillance at the workplace, while employees who use the Internet at work stand a 33 percent chance of being exposed to *constant* surveillance.[11] Even employees who engage in hard, unrewarding manual labor, such as hotel housekeeping, are subject to electronic scrutiny and performance monitoring. During a recent hotel stay, one of us was puzzled that the housekeeping person assigned to his room was visibly upset when he told her she didn't need to clean the room. She knocked on the door once more and asked if she could use the phone. As she picked up the receiver, she explained that she had to enter her code into the room's phone so management would give her credit for making up that room. The telephone surveillance system was gathering metrics about the number of rooms cleaned, how fast they were cleaned, and which worker was doing the cleaning. If guests complained, blame would be easy to assign. Likewise, it's not difficult to imagine that these data were being used to discipline—or "motivate"—workers who cleaned too slowly. Some hotels even track their housekeeping staff's productivity with a cell phone app that measures movement and speed at all times.[12] If workers stand still or sit down for even a few seconds, management knows.

"This Call May Be Monitored"

Of all service-sector jobs, call centers push workplace surveillance to the extreme. These jobs often crush workers together in a honeycomb of cubicles with almost no privacy: bosses and coworkers can hear you amid the din of voices, can see you over the low walls, and can track your minute-by-minute productivity score on LCD monitors.[13] The electronic surveillance extends much further, too. At most call centers, such as the ones operated by Time Warner Cable, expectations are broken down second by second: "2 minutes, 30 seconds—average length of call; 16 seconds—the maximum time a customer can be left on hold; 8 seconds—the time to complete paperwork between calls. Simply finding time to go to the bathroom can be tough."[14] Your phone must be active at almost all times, typically with only five to twenty seconds allowed between calls.[15] In telemarketing call centers, automated systems called "predictive dialing" increase pressure further by automatically dialing the next call as soon as the last one is terminated, pushing work-ers to achieve on-phone rates of up to fifty-four minutes each hour.[16] Of course, managers can listen to your conversations in real time to see if you have a friendly tone of voice and are technically competent,[17] but evaluation of your performance can happen retrospectively too, because all calls are recorded and archived; all e-mails and computer keystrokes are saved; just about everything you do, in fact, is instantly converted into "data."[18]

All this is done in the name of efficiency, just as Taylor proposed, but the experience is grueling for workers. Indeed, "e-slave" has entered the urban slang lexicon to describe call-center employees who put up with tremendous stress, work long hours, and have unpredictable sched-ules.[19] Some workers refer to the call-center performance systems as a "technological whip" that automates the slave driver's task, contribut-ing to a general climate that includes "bullying, impossible sales targets, not receiving wages on time, and hostility to unions."[20] Given this harsh environment, some call centers have an annual turnover rate of over 100 percent.[21]

And managers are constantly on the lookout for ways to increase output, even if it pushes workers to the breaking point.[22] At a tech sup-port call center operated by the Charles Schwab brokerage firm, one worker related: "A year ago we had three minutes after each call to write up what happened. That was called 'wrap.' Now there's no wrap time; we have to write notes as we handle calls."[23] To cope with this labor inten-sification, employees must shift that time on to customers; one worker at a different call center explains:

What you end up doing is keeping the client on the phone while you enter your notes, which makes an already annoyed customer become even more annoyed. And doing that is just a charade—you're wasting the customer's time just so you can avoid getting a "hit" [being disciplined] for refusing an inbound ring.[24]

"Your Call Is Important to Us"
Have you ever felt that your call wasn't taken in the order received? Well, you were right. "Customer relationship management" (CRM) systems triage calls in order of importance based on how valuable you are as a customer. If you fit the right demographic, are calling from the right area code, buy a lot, or

seldom complain—all of that is logged in your profile, and you might be given preferential treatment because of it. Or if you're not in a valued category, you could be stuck forever in the purgatory of phone-tree mazes and on-hold music. CRMs are social sorting systems par excellence: they're automated, invisible, and discriminatory. Now government offices also use them to manage their customers/citizens.[25]

Performance Monitoring

Performance monitoring can be found just about everywhere these days, with the use of wireless order-entry systems to monitor servers in restaurants, GPS devices to track truck drivers, or databases to evaluate the productivity of professors. What does performance monitoring mean to the people involved? From management's perspective, it's a mechanism for achieving efficiency, accountability, and quality. It also implies the ability to make decisions, especially disciplinary decisions, based on the results gathered. As the Institute for Management Excellence puts it, "It is a fact of life that employee performance monitoring, discipline and dealing with employee issues is part of a manager's job—it actually defines what a manager is: someone who has the authority to hire, fire and discipline."[26]

From the perspective of nonmanagement employees, performance monitoring means that workers are subject to varying degrees of surveillance and must strive to prove their worth. It's a fancy way of saying they must work harder and compete for scarce resources to have any chance at job security, raises, or promotions. It implies a state of insecurity for most employees and a lack of trust by managers. At its worst, performance monitoring can create a hostile workplace; at its best, it can allow for structured feedback and improved performance. Either way, like other forms of surveillance, it's always an expression of power.

Performance-monitoring systems shape human behavior and action. As we noted in the first chapter, technologies guide what is considered possible and desirable. With a critical lens, we can "read" technologies to see what values they possess and what types of relationships they produce: Competition or cooperation? Suspicion or trust? Hierarchy or equality? At a very basic level, of course, performance-monitoring regimes are antithetical to the value of human autonomy—the underlying premise of such surveillance is that humans can't be counted on to self-regulate and work productively without close bureaucratic supervision. In this way, performance monitoring normalizes hierarchical relationships between managers and workers. It makes it *seem* natural that management should constantly monitor and evaluate employees or that managers should have power over others in the workplace. That these statements probably sound obvious shows how persuasive this particular management paradigm has been. In comparison, the idea of a more democratic workplace, whether through collective bargaining with labor unions or simply through a more egalitarian structure, may sound idealistic or inefficient, especially to American readers, even though plenty of workplaces thrive under such models.[27]

Performance monitoring also feeds the illusion that the criteria used to evaluate employees are objective and unbiased, even when there are many standards for evaluating work (e.g., quantity, quality, creativity, effectiveness, customer satisfaction, teamwork, safety, employee happiness). One unfortunate effect of widespread performance monitoring is that it allows the criteria of competition, speed, and efficiency to outweigh others that might be just as good or even better, such as cooperation, trust, meaningful participation, or care. This subordination of alternative criteria is bad enough for most jobs, because it can diminish workers' satisfaction and investment.[28] And in professions intended to help others, such as teaching or nursing, performance monitoring and other forms of Tayloristic surveillance may have even more harmful effects. Let's take a closer look.

A Day with Nurse Betty: Hospital Tracking Systems

Nurse Betty has a problem. She cares deeply about her patients and wants to give them the attention they need to get better and not feel frightened or lonely. But hospitals don't make money by giving this kind of care; they make money by keeping all their beds full, running procedures, assigning patients the bare minimum of nurse support, and quickly discharging them once the profitable tests are done and it's safe for them to leave—and sometimes before it's safe. By speeding up "throughput" in this way, like factories, and by running a lot of tests, hospitals can maximize the billing potential for each patient.[29]

Nurses at Betty's hospital, and at many others, had creatively resisted management's drive for increased patient throughput. One way they did this was to pretend patients were still in the hospital even after they'd been discharged. That way new patients wouldn't be loaded in quite so quickly. Fewer patients to take care of meant more time could be spent with each patient. Being responsible for fewer patients also meant nurses didn't feel quite so frenzied, stressed, and burned-out. This coping mechanism was possible because Betty and her colleagues had to enter data into a computer system when a patient was discharged so the room could be cleaned and made ready for the next patient. If nurses delayed entering these data, it would effectively slow down admissions and reduce the number of patients under their care.[30]

But hospital administrators have installed new surveillance systems to make sure Betty and others cooperate with the assembly line. One is a bed management system that relies on radio-frequency identification (RFID) tags for patients. Embedded in a patient's wristband, the small RFID chip is automatically scanned when it passes detectors at the hospital exits. As soon as the wristband leaves the hospital, presumably on a patient, the bed management system is triggered to update that patient's room status to "empty" and send an alert so housekeeping staff can clean the room. Thus new patients are admitted quickly, and nurses are forced to adapt. In a constant battle over control of the workplace, some nurses have responded by removing patients' wristbands and leaving them in the rooms. The danger is that this maneuver more clearly constitutes intentional circumventing of the system rather than simply "forgetting" to update the room status in the system.[31] Thus nurses who do this are more easily disciplined.

Meanwhile, on another floor, hospital emergency departments worry about admitting *too many* patients or admitting patients who aren't sick enough. Because only so many beds are available, it's better for them to be occupied by the sickest patients so that care can go to the neediest and hospitals can generate the most revenue. It's a tough balance: if hospitals have empty beds they make less money, but if all their beds are full, they may have to divert needy patients to other hospitals (or have them waiting on stretchers in hallways), which is not good. So physicians in emergency departments are subjected to routine performance monitoring and pressure to admit fewer patients. One hospital administrator explained:

We monitor all the activity of all our docs. We give them reports every month on their acuity, their time to disposition, the number of tests per doctor per diagnosis, their efficiency in terms of what we pay through the department, and that's all recorded. And your abilities, your bonuses, all that information is used as a 360[-degree] view of you as an emergency physician in the department. But if you're admitting twenty-two percent or twenty-three percent, twenty-four percent, then . . . you should be more tight with your admissions because you're actually losing [the hospital] money. . . . The chairman would say, "You know, the last couple months you've been admitting a lot more percentiles. Just try to bring it down a little bit."[32]

Perhaps because of their high professional status, physicians are probably more often given incentives to admit fewer patients rather than punished for admitting too many. Still, performance monitoring can serve as public shaming, because monthly reports typically include names alongside performance scores.

Another hospital surveillance system relies on RFID tags worn by the staff. Under the Tayloristic name "workflow management," administrators use these tags to track the movements and locations of staff in real time. The ostensible goal is to reduce redundant movements, minimize inventory, and "rationalize" hospitals so they are as efficient as possible.[33] While all that sounds smart and practical, surveillance is always about control, so the people under its gaze seldom see it in such a positive light.

What ends up happening is that hospital administrators can't help but discipline workers whose locations are being tracked. In one case a hospital was just piloting a workflow management system and asked staff to wear RFID-embedded badges. An administrator saw that two orderlies, people who transport patients, were hanging out at a loading dock, so he called them on their walkie-talkies and asked where they were. When they both lied about their locations, the administrator stormed down to the loading dock and fired them on the spot.[34] The intended purpose of the system was to improve efficiency, and workers were never told they'd be spied on, but once the system was in place it was automatically transformed into a disciplinary surveillance technology.

Although various tracking and performance-monitoring systems in hospitals may improve some measures of productivity, they may also produce unintended consequences that burden workers and their patients. If their primary goals are to increase throughput and save (or make) money, then the health care mission of these organizations may suffer. Then again, many people and communities may suffer if hospitals go out of business, so the problems are much deeper and more complex than simply saying no to workplace surveillance and yes to care and compassion. Nonetheless, many hospital staff find tracking systems unreasonably invasive and feel they diminish autonomy and trust in the workplace.[35] Some nurses even intentionally smash RFID tags and sabotage the systems.[36] It stands to reason that authentically involving workers in decision making and organizing workplaces to provide incentives instead of punishments would boost morale and combat arbitrary abuses of power.

Cheers!

Bartending may look like fun, but every drink bartenders pour can be scrutinized by RFID-enabled pour spouts and wireless surveillance systems. Want to give someone a bigger shot for a better tip? Don't try it with these systems in place. They send information about what drink was poured, by whom, at what time, how many ounces were poured and how many ounces should have been poured. There are even systems for regulating the pouring of draft beers. According to one bar owner: "My staff know their every move is being watched. If they are doing their jobs well, I will see it. If they need a tune up I will see it. Even if I see things days later I can go back to the archives and get all the detail I need."[37] As if dealing with a bunch of drunken people weren't hard enough.

The "Eyes in the Sky" at Casinos

One of our students was a blackjack dealer at a casino. She described the elaborate rituals she had to perform for the invisible security staff watching her through cameras mounted above her table. She had to ensure that her hand of cards was never lifted more than forty-five degrees off the table; she had to position the deck at a precise angle to the edge of the table; she couldn't touch her cards or the deck unnecessarily, because it might be construed as a signal to a player; when she accepted tips, she had to tap the chips against the table and immediately place them in her tip container; and when she left the table, she had to clap her hands together and turn them palm up for the cameras to see. Any deviation from protocol would automatically trigger an inspection from security that could result in disciplinary action.

Casinos are test beds for cutting-edge, integrated surveillance systems. Because of the tens of billions of dollars in profits they make each year,[38] they're supercharged with systems many government agencies only dream about. It's not just the dealers who are being watched—it's everyone. As one director of surveillance puts it, "There's nowhere on the casino floor that you can hide."[39] When people walk into a casino, the video cameras quickly process images of them through a facial recognition system that determines whether they are in a database of restricted customers.[40] If they are, staff in the security room will radio down to security personnel on the floor to escort them off the premises. Even smaller casinos tend to have over a thousand cameras, some that remain stationary over tables and many that can pan, tilt, and zoom to follow people.[41]

In addition to elaborate camera systems and facial recognition technologies, casinos now have a way to track chips by embedding radio-frequency identification tags in every one of them. These "smart chips" can then be used on "intelligent tables" to track the exact bets of every player, determine the players' value so they can be "comped" for drinks or shows if they're high rollers, and deter the theft or counterfeiting of chips.[42] Security staff can automatically count and audit chips to make it harder for cashiers to steal. There are already prototypes in the works for RFID-embedded cards, but until they're adopted there are other ways to monitor gamblers' hands: "A new technology from MindPlay reads invisible codes on cards as they're dealt from the shoe. The system knows, in real time, what players are holding and betting. Casinos can snare card counters by comparing their play with known counting strategies."[43] The goal is total transparency. And because casino employees are involved in an estimated 34 percent of all instances of theft or cheating, they're watched very closely.[44]

Of course, surveillance doesn't rely entirely on technologies. The technologies are complemented by nested systems of people watching people: inspectors watch dealers; pit bosses watch inspectors; floor managers watch pit bosses; security staff watch everyone from another room; and they are watched by other security staff at remote locations.[45] Besides deterring theft, some of the control functions are designed to make workers more accommodating to clientele. For instance, dealers are expected to have "outgoing personalities," put up with flirtation, and encourage players to make higher bets.[46] Similarly, waitresses in casinos are monitored to make sure they act as "objects of desire" by dressing suggestively and flattering gamblers; if waitresses don't cooperate, bartenders slow down their drink orders so they receive worse tips.[47] It shouldn't be unexpected that the "eyes in the sky" at casinos would support voyeurism, objectification, and control of others—that's exactly what they're designed to do.

Corporate Espionage

Jerry Treppel thought someone was going through his trash at night, but he wasn't sure, so he hired a private investigator. The PI hid behind a fence all night and, sure enough, saw two men take Treppel's trash away and put decoy replacement trash back in the cans. As the men drove off in a gray minivan, the detective discreetly followed them and then tracked down their identities. The trash stealers were private investigators too! They were hired by the Biovail Corporation, a Canadian pharmaceutical company that Treppel was suing for allegedly damaging his career.[48] (Treppel was a securities analyst at an investment firm. When he advised investors to sell Biovail stock, that company insisted he be reprimanded. Soon after, he was fired.[49]) Hiring PIs is just one of the many surveillance tactics corporations use to spy on individuals, other companies, and governments. Welcome to the world of corporate espionage.

In another telling case a few years ago, the technology company Hewlett-Packard (HP) got into a lot of trouble for hiring private investigators who had little respect for the law. Patricia Dunn, then chair of HP's board of directors, had a problem with board members' leaking secrets to the media. To find the culprits, she hired a firm of private investigators that supposedly hired another company to engage in the seedy practice of "pretexting." Pretexting is an identity theft technique of calling a company, such as a bank or public utility, and pretending to be someone else so you can get access to private information. In this instance PIs got the Social Security numbers and phone records for more than twenty-four people, including HP board members, other employees, and nine reporters.[50] One PI changed a reporter's cell phone password so he could listen to her messages and scrutinize her call log without her interrupting.[51] Patricia Dunn and others involved were fired and charged with four felony counts. A California judge, who was evidently soft on (corporate) crime, dismissed the charges.[52]

What's probably most remarkable is that these examples were made public at all. Companies engage in corporate espionage all the time. They want to discover trade secrets. They want to know who's leaking sensitive information. They want to know what their competitors are doing. They want to figure out who's counterfeiting their products.[53] They want to know a lot, and they're sometimes willing to transgress ethical and legal boundaries. Employees may thus be the unwitting targets of surveillance by other companies or by their own.

Because corporate espionage is commonplace, private investigators are busier than ever. Close to sixty thousand PIs are licensed in the United States, and who knows how many more are unlicensed.[54] Some of the corporate spies are even current, active-duty CIA agents who are granted permission by the agency to "moonlight" at private companies.[55] And the spying isn't just on behalf of high-powered technology and pharmaceutical companies. The entertainment industry, the insurance industry, the chemical industry—they all do it. Even the circus industry has been involved with hiring PIs to infiltrate People for the Ethical Treatment of Animals and other animal rights groups.[56] Espionage is now a key risk management technique used by many companies.

For most employees, this just adds one more layer of (potential) surveillance to their lives. In addition to companies' running background checks before hiring people, monitoring their electronic communications, and subjecting them to performance monitoring, employers and their competitors may be digging through workers' trash or accessing their phone records. It may be next to impossible for individuals to protect themselves. According to one private investigator, "If someone is willing to break the law to get your personal info, there's almost nothing you can do to prevent them."[57] In the summer of 2011, the world discovered just how true this was when we learned that major newspapers were hiring private investigators to tap into the voice-mail systems of celebrities, killed British soldiers, high-profile crime victims, and members of the royal family.[58]

The New Ford: Drug Testing and Moral Management

Early in this chapter, we saw that Henry Ford had a special department monitoring the home lives of his employees to ensure that they were living up to his moral standards. He believed that the ideal workers didn't just get the job done; they lived their personal lives as the Ford Motor Company preferred. These days this sort of corporate paternalism is frowned on as overreaching—most of us expect that if we do a good job while we're on the clock, the rest of our lives belong to us.

But do they? We've given several examples of the ways contemporary surveillance is used by businesses in their attempt to reduce risk and successfully manage their workforce. Credit checks see if potential employees are good with their money. Background checks search not only for arrests or convictions, but also for past use of workers' compensation or lawsuits. In many workplaces, regulations prohibit hiring smokers, while "wellness programs" give special encouragements to those who work out in the company gym or pursue other healthful lifestyle choices. It may not be enough that you're a whiz at programming—you may need to be a healthy, nonsmoking, exercising, debt-free programmer with a clean legal history and no record of using workers' compensation.

One now commonplace example of this invasive management is the drug-testing frenzy that emerged back in the 1980s. Testing job applicants, employees, welfare clients, and even students typically can be done with relatively low-cost kits that analyze a urine sample to detect evidence of drug use. These tests measure certain residues left in the body *long after* drug use. Because of this quirk in the technology, drug-testing programs provide no evidence regarding current intoxication or impairment. Instead, they implement a 24/7/365 monitoring program on what employees take into their bodies—a far more encompassing version of Henry Ford's inspections of his employees' homes.

If it weren't for all the human pain, wasted money, and nasty politics, the saga of workplace drug testing might be a comedy rather than the tragedy it is. The movement began with a passion during the Reagan administration's War on Drugs of the 1980s. The push to test the urine of America's blue-collar workers was ready-made for the politics of the era. As part of the War on Drugs, workplace drug testing deputized America's employers as quasi-government enforcers of drug control laws. It included overblown claims that America's workers were stoned; it put labor unions in the position of seeming to defend workers' right to be stoned; and it offered a dramatic expansion of employers' power over employees as the moralist commands followed workers home for the weekend and on their vacations. Finally, it meant a huge new stream of revenue for America's pharmaceutical industry, a perennial heavyweight in campaign contributions.[59]

Drug-testing technology was first developed in prisons and the military. The next wave of the rollout was in safety-sensitive positions like pilots, train crews, law enforcement, and power plant personnel. Job applicants were brought into the game when prices dropped on low-quality screening tests, and then in some areas those who applied for public assistance were required to demonstrate their abstinence. Along the way, high school students got in on the fun as some districts began testing athletes and anyone else who participated in school-sponsored activities.[60]

Yet this sort of testing for illegal drug use just doesn't make a lot of sense. The most damaging drug in the American workforce is alcohol, which is almost never tested for and was never part of the American debate over drugs in the workplace. Another puzzle is that most drug tests are best at detecting signs of marijuana, which can stay in the body for weeks after use, while evidence of more serious drugs disappears more quickly. So employee drug testing basically skipped the serious stuff to give corporations the power to examine the marijuana smoking habits of their off-duty employees. Add in that drug tests don't even measure current impairment—only past use—and we've got some pretty major disconnects in the safety-testing rationale. The almost silly, unnecessary intrusion of these surveillance policies drives home a point we see in several parts of this book: surveillance doesn't always make sense from a technical, rational, problem-solving perspective. Sometimes it seems to be about power for power's sake or inspired by other motives that wouldn't stand the scrutiny of public discussion.

Checking You Out

Chances are good that if you apply for a job, your prospective employers will try to dig up some dirt on you. They may call your references, request credit reports, or—as we've mentioned—run criminal background checks. They'll probably Google you too. Additionally, 75 percent of US companies now conduct formal searches of applicants' online activity, and 70 percent admit rejecting candidates based on the information they've found.[61]

Some entrepreneurial companies have sprung up to help employers run online background checks. Social Intelligence is one of the big ones, and it claims to do "deep" web searches on individuals, tapping into social networking sites, blogs, Tumblr, Craigslist, Yahoo! groups, and many, many more sites.[62] They've even received the blessing of the Federal Trade Commission to archive *all* social networking posts for seven years.[63] So cleaning up your Facebook page a few months before applying for a job won't help because seven years of posts may already be on file, ready to be mined for any compromising tidbits.

Some of the things they say they look for are sexually explicit photos or videos, racist remarks, or evidence of illegal activity. But there's also a gray area of subjective indicators they may use to weed out candidates: things like making inappropriate comments, holding marginal political views, or having a questionable lifestyle.[64] The chief executive of Social Intelligence says, for instance, that a red flag was raised by a photo of someone next to some large marijuana plants in a greenhouse.[65] While we can easily see that this is not evidence of "illegal activity," it was suggestive enough to eliminate that person as a candidate. Another person belonged to a Facebook group supporting the exclusive use of the English language in the United States.[66] While we may not agree with this position, it isn't evidence that the person would treat non-English-speaking people differently—indeed, belonging to a "group" isn't even proof that a person believes in that position. Discrimination against prospective employees can take many forms, however, and some are perfectly legal. Currently, for example, employers shouldn't ask (or search for information) about your race, age, religion, marital status, or disabilities, but federal employment law doesn't prohibit them from asking about your sexual orientation.[67]

Finally, don't think employers will stop watching your online activity once you're hired. Social Intelligence also offers ongoing monitoring of all employee posts, photos, videos, and groups and serves up "near real-time notifications and alerts" to supervisors.[68] So if someone tagged you in a questionable photo over the weekend, you might be fired for it on Monday morning. Think of it as Workplace Surveillance 2.0.

Back Talk

Now a high-priced man does just what he's told to do, and no back talk. Do you understand that? —FREDERICK WINSLOW TAYLOR[69]

It is a degradation of human beings, Damn You.
—An American worker, commenting on urine-based drug testing[70]

Despite Taylor's hope, back talk has been a big part of the story of workplace surveillance. A lot of resistance these days occurs on the Internet on blogs, websites, and other "rant" forums, which is one reason companies are monitoring these media. In an era where corporations try desperately to control their public image, companies see online venting by workers as a real threat that may damage profitability and perhaps even put them out of business. And there are an overwhelming number of "workplace sucks" sites: WalmartSucks, RadioShackSucks, HomeDepotSucks, and thousands more.[71] It's not clear whether such sites have been effective at reducing workplace surveillance, and they may have increased it (as companies monitor the sites and try to shut them down), but they do offer a public venue for griping, outing unsavory corporate practices, or whistle-blowing. They also provide a medium for isolated workers to join together and collectively push for policy changes.[72]

In a more traditional vein, labor unions have been at the forefront of political struggles over such things as employee drug-testing programs, new means of tracking employees' locations, call and keystroke monitoring, and test-based assessments of teacher performance. In our discussions of ID cards and schools, we looked at the quiet, everyday resistance to surveillance that individuals practice in their lives. But here we're going to note that the politics of surveillance also include some prominent public battles that end up in courts and legislatures.

It's no surprise that workers fight back against surveillance—so do corporations when they oppose regulatory inspection and government agencies when they fight "sunshine" laws. Surveillance is an expression of power that reduces autonomy and expands the visibility of our actions—people and organizations typically have a strong interest in opposing intensified scrutiny. In much of the surveillance covered in this book, the people targeted are not well positioned to fight back. Consumers, for example, are not typically shopping as an organized group, so they lack the information and collective clout to do much about anything. Students, criminal suspects, drivers, job applicants, and others typically find themselves in the same lonely and powerless boat.

But unionized workers have been a particularly strong source of opposition to increasing surveillance. By pressuring legislators, filing lawsuits, and working with regulatory agencies, unions have been able to at least publicize and modify, if not fully prevent, increases in the surveillance of their workers. Working with more specialized groups— like the American Civil Liberties Union, the Electronic Privacy Information Center, and Privacy International—unions try to play the role that privacy regulators and agencies tend to neglect, especially in the United States. With US labor unions declining in membership and political influence, one of the most effective forms of political opposition to surveillance may be disappearing. It remains to be seen whether online tools and social media can pick up the slack and slow—or roll back—the seemingly inexorable push of workplace surveillance.

Conclusion

Like schools, the typical workplace is defined by the struggle to manage large numbers of people. In each environment, one group attempts to exert power over others. And in each environment, too, the new arsenal of the surveillance society is redefining our daily lives. With performance monitoring, cubicle farms, keystroke tracking, background checks, drug testing, and all the other facets of surveillance in the modern workplace, the trends most famously linked to Frederick Winslow Taylor have become a way of life. Older means of surveillance such as audits, double-entry bookkeeping, time clocks, and simply concentrating workers in single, observable locations now seem like quaint throwbacks to a simpler era.

6: Security at Any Cost?

Don't Touch My Junk

- Thomas Sawyer was mortified as the urine from his damaged urostomy bag spilled onto his shirt and ran down his leg. The TSA agent was evidently overzealous in applying the new "enhanced pat-down" to Sawyer, who just wanted to catch his flight, not become a spectacle at the airport screening station. Sawyer commented afterward: "I'm a good American. I know why we're doing this [airport screening], and I understand it. . . . But this was extremely embarrassing, and it didn't have to happen. With educated TSA workers, it wouldn't have happened."[1]

- An employee of ABC News also reported undergoing a humiliating search in 2010 at the hands of a TSA agent in the days before Thanksgiving. She related: "The woman who checked me reached her hands inside my underwear and felt her way around. . . . It was basically worse than going to the gynecologist. It was embarrassing. It was demeaning. It was inappropriate."[2]

- John Tyner gained media fame when he decided to protest the deployment of full-body scanners and aggressive pat-downs at US airports. Before the required search could commence, he told the TSA agent, "If you touch my junk, I'm going to have you arrested."[3] Tyner himself was detained and threatened with a fine of $10,000, but his covert cell phone recording of that interaction made headlines and helped spark a short-lived "opt out" movement of people refusing to undergo full-body scans.[4] For the cause, some people even stripped down and walked around airports in Speedos.[5]

Let's face it: it's rare for Americans to publicly protest national security provisions, and it's even more unusual for the mainstream media to run stories when trouble erupts. After the terrorist attacks of September 11, 2001, most Americans readily complied with a series of new government security programs. But it struck a nerve when airports began enhanced pat-downs and electronic strip searches using full-body scanners, which can peer through clothing.

As you know, a lot of contemporary surveillance is abstract and remote, at least initially. It's a bunch of computers collecting, sharing, and manipulating data. Usually you don't even know it's going on. But there's nothing abstract about someone grabbing your crotch. And many people find it invasive and inappropriate for strangers to scrutinize their naked bodies, even if those people are far away and the images are blurred. Another dimension to this, of course, is that many travelers might not object in principle to random searches or even to profiling, but they find it insulting that *they* would be chosen for systematic, intensive screening.

Still, most people just go along with it. They say things like, "If that's what you have to do to keep us safe, that's what you have to do."[6] The assumption is, first off, that government surveillance and security programs *are* keeping us safe. Second, people apparently believe there is a necessary trade-off between security and liberty, or security and privacy—that an increase in one means a decrease in the other. Third, as the sentiment of "that's what you have to do to be safe" illustrates, efforts to protect people from terrorist attacks are ranked higher than any other forms of protection—whether protection from illegal and degrading searches, from radiation from full-body scanners, or from the specter of an increasingly powerful and totalizing security infrastructure.

It's a scary world out there: terrorists, hostile nations, criminals, drug traffickers, environmental disasters, economic crises, pandemic diseases, and much more. All these threats contribute to our culture of insecurity. In the face of these insecurities, we embrace nearly anything that promises to keep us safe. With each crisis or media panic, we take another giant leap into the surveillance society. This chapter explores spreading methods of surveillance in areas like border control, policing, and airport security. We'll suggest that there is little evidence that surveillance actually makes us safer. This often puzzling world of surveillance and security raises challenging questions about the roles of politics, industry, and the mass media in creating a world that appears so frightening that comprehensive surveillance seems the only sane response.

Exclusionary Security Systems at the Airport

We're surrounded by security systems, and not just the screening devices at airports or the video cameras in parking lots. The locks on our doors, the alarm systems in our homes, and the walls around some of our communities all protect us from harm in some way. Security is fundamental to how societies are organized. Historically, people gravitated to cities for economic opportunity and sought protection from invaders by building city walls and posting sentries. Similarly, political theorists argue that nation-states were formed in part to keep citizens safe from outsiders. But in trying to achieve security, one must always make decisions about who belongs and who doesn't, which means security is exclusionary by design.

These days our security systems are increasingly electronic and automated. The latest gadgets and gizmos—from antivirus software to facial recognition cameras—are used to identify threats, protect people, and safeguard property. Although that's not necessarily a bad thing, it does mean people are placing a lot of faith in technologies to work, often without much evidence. Additionally, automated (or partially automated) systems obscure the social exclusions inherent in security, which can make biases seem natural or nonexistent unless you're the one being discriminated against.

If you're singled out as a security threat, you may never find out why. You'll also have a hard time correcting your "risk" designation in the system. For instance, no-fly lists are notorious for false positives whereby innocent people are routinely questioned at airports or excluded from flying altogether. One Canadian man got so fed up with repeatedly being interrogated by agents and missing his flights that he changed his legal name (from Mario Labbé to François Mario Labbé) just to avoid future complications. It worked.[7] Civil rights organizations have been vocal in pointing out that there appears to be racial and religious profiling in the compiling of vast no-fly lists and terrorist watch lists, which include over 1 million names and are growing all the time.[8]

Some notable figures who have been included on US no-fly lists include Nelson Mandela, the former South African president and recipient of the Nobel Peace Prize, and the late US senator Edward Kennedy. Kennedy complained directly to Department of Homeland Security secretary Tom Ridge to get his name removed from the list. But since most people don't have a direct line to the DHS secretary, they have to try the bureaucratic Traveler Redress Inquiry Program and hope for the best. Homeland Security no-fly lists work by amassing data on travelers and potential travelers, automatically comparing passenger names with no-fly lists, and flagging passengers who "match" the names on the list so that they can be stopped, detained, or compelled to prove they aren't really the ones thought to be a threat. In other words, the system doesn't just silently collect data; it also intervenes to control mobility. Even travelers who don't experience any difficulty with such systems might be disturbed to learn that their personal details (name, age, address, credit card number, emergency contact information, cell phone number, political opinions, sexual orientation, health information) will be saved in the US system for at least fifteen years—something people in the European Union are especially troubled by because their laws put a five-year limit on saving such data.[9]

Security systems can involve hidden prejudices too. For instance, facial recognition systems can have more trouble identifying the sex of people from Asian ethnic groups than Caucasians, and some "smart" cameras will even ask if someone was blinking when they try to snap a picture of an Asian person.[10] Iris scans, used at US borders, tend to work better with blue eyes and often fail at achieving matches for elderly people, who may have cataracts or normal changes in eye structure.[11] People who have visual impairments or must use wheelchairs will similarly have trouble getting by such airport screening and identification systems. Other biometric systems have a hard time identifying "black" faces.[12]

It's important to talk about the built-in biases of these security systems because the systems are often pitched as neutral alternatives to screening by humans. This is especially salient in light of the numerous complaints about racial and religious profiling by airport security personnel. A government report found that "67 percent of the passengers subjected to personal searches upon entering the United States were people of color" and that "black women are more likely than any other U.S. citizens to be strip-searched."[13] If you are routinely targeted for additional searches while other people are fast-tracked through the system, it might not matter much whether the bias resides in a human being or in a computer code.

And some people really are fast-tracked through airports and other border crossings. For instance, the NEXUS program is a "preclearance" program that allows eligible US and Canadian travelers to move rapidly across border checkpoints between these countries. People fill out an application for the NEXUS program, undergo background checks, submit to a brief interview, pay $50, scan their irises for biometric identification, and are given an RFID-embedded card that can be used as a substitute for a passport.[14] That's right—no passport is needed to cross the border. When people with NEXUS cards arrive at an immigration inspection area, they can go straight to a kiosk where they swipe their cards and look into a lens that scans their irises to match their identity. Poof! They're free to cross while the rest of us move slowly through the snaking lines and prepare to play twenty questions with a dour border agent . . . or worse.

Dangerous Borders

Thermal sensors, motion detectors, and video cameras punctuate the desert landscape. In addition to the ever-expanding cordon of twenty-foot fences and barbed wire, high-tech surveillance systems integrate seamlessly into border control infrastructures, helping agents prevent unlawful entry into the United States. That was the vision anyhow. In 2011 the United States scrapped its Secure Border Initiative network (SBInet), disappointed that Boeing had blown through an almost billion-dollar budget only to fail in achieving the dream of a technology-fortified border between the United States and Mexico.[15] The SBInet "virtual fence" stalled after covering only fifty-three out of two thousand miles of the US southern border, and the implemented technology was glitchy and unreliable.[16] This is just one example of a pattern seen in a global security industry that blossomed after 9/11 and has consistently profited from lucrative contracts with very little effective follow-through.[17]

Nonetheless, US borders remain riddled with surveillance. There are now 20,500 border agents and 1,200 National Guard troops policing the border—a massive human surveillance force.[18] As one might expect, these government personnel do use video cameras, ID-checking systems, drug-sniffing dogs, RFID scanners for precleared vehicles, and even unmanned aerial drones, which we'll discuss in the next section.

Get in on the Action?

The state of Texas has a website called the Texas Virtual Border Watch that encourages people to monitor webcams remotely, from the comfort of their own homes, and report suspicious activities to law enforcement by e-mail.[19] In this way, authorities attempt to enroll the public in border surveillance and cultivate support for border fortification, which they say is designed to "deny drug and human smugglers unobserved access to the U.S."[20]

Members of controversial citizen groups like the Minuteman Project and American Border Control have also taken it upon themselves to patrol border areas in attempts to spot undocumented immigrants and report them to the authorities. Using binoculars, night-vision goggles, drones, and other surveillance equipment, members of such groups set up camp in forbidding environments like the Arizona desert just north of Nogales.[21] The Minuteman Project in particular has drawn a lot of criticism for its extreme nativist position and vigilante tactics, which include the apparent unlawful imprisonment of immigrants.[22] In turn, other groups like the American Civil Liberties Union (ACLU) have taken to monitoring the vigilante groups to ensure that they don't violate the rights of immigrants.

One of the most consistent outcomes of surveillance based in a single location is that it pushes people elsewhere to avoid detection. The fortification of border areas in California and Texas has produced a funnel effect so that undocumented immigrants now tend to cross the border at some of its most dangerous places, including the harsh Arizona desert, resulting in hundreds of deaths each year.[23] This has catalyzed a different kind of surveillance by humanitarian organizations seeking to prevent border deaths. The group Humane Borders, for instance, has used global positioning systems and geographic information systems to map the locations where clusters of deaths have occurred and erect water stations in those areas. Each of the more than one hundred water stations maintained by this organization is "stocked with a 100-gallon water tank, food, clothing, and first-aid kits" and marked by "a blue flag flown from a thirty-foot pole."[24] Humane Borders has also produced high-resolution maps of dangerous border areas, locations of water stations, and emergency phone numbers and distributed these maps to communities in Mexico. One remarkable finding is that border agents have tacit agreements with humanitarian groups not to patrol directly around water stations; otherwise migrants will be more likely to avoid these lifesaving resources and perhaps die.[25]

There are many other manifestations of border surveillance. In 2003 the European Union implemented the EURODAC system to collect fingerprints and other information from individuals seeking asylum. When refugees arrive in an EU country, that country is charged with collecting biometric data on those over fourteen years old and sharing that information with all partner EU countries as well as Iceland, Norway, and Switzerland. People whose fingerprints are already in the system will be routed to the first country that fingerprinted them.[26]

While the initial intentions behind EURODAC may have been reasonable, the system oversimplifies the plight of refugees and tosses some of them into legal limbo. After all, people fleeing persecution in their home countries may not have the documents necessary to prove citizenship. So how can they prove their citizenship in a country that may be persecuting people who come from certain ethnic backgrounds or hold the wrong religious or political beliefs? One solution border officials have come up with is to give asylum seekers "citizenship tests," asking people from Sierra Leone, for instance, "What is the name of the largest shopping street in Freetown?"[27] If you come from a small village, have never been to Freetown, or aren't affluent enough to shop, you may fail such a test, which means you probably won't be granted asylum and won't be sent back to your home country either. Some people just drift in such cases, living on the margins of society, but others wind up in immigrant detention facilities where they may be held for years with little legal recourse.[28] There are even reports of immigrants' intentionally infecting themselves with HIV in order to be granted asylum in countries like France, which has rules about not deporting people with life-threatening illnesses that can't be treated appropriately in their home countries (unlike the United States, which automatically turns away immigrants with HIV).[29]

Like most surveillance systems, EURODAC has morphed since its inception, expanding its uses through function creep. When it was initially conceived, safeguards ensured that fingerprints would be used only to see if the person had previously filed for asylum.[30] This was done because under the privacy laws of some member countries, such as France and the Netherlands, it was illegal to collect fingerprints from people who weren't criminal suspects. In 2009, however, these constraints were relaxed in the name of fighting terrorism and serious crime.[31]

It's a Bird. It's a Plane. It's a . . . Drone?

A pilot of an unmanned aerial vehicle (UAV) or "drone" sits in front of a video screen at March Air Reserve Base in California. He skillfully guides his Predator drone to hover over suspected insurgents in Iraq, nearly seven thousand miles away, and fires an air-to-ground Hellfire missile at the targets, killing them all. Then he packs up for the day and goes to his son's soccer game.[32]

Drones are the next big thing in security-oriented surveillance, not just in war zones but also along borders, over farms, and in cities in the United States, the United Kingdom, and elsewhere. The US military and the CIA have embraced drones as essential weapons in the "war on terror" and have flown tens of thousands of missions and launched hundreds of missile attacks in Iraq, Afghanistan, and Pakistan.[33] The two main types of drones are the MQ-1 Predator, which is best suited for constant overhead surveillance but is also often equipped with missiles, and the more advanced MQ-9 Reaper, which is "designed to go after time-sensitive targets with persistence and precision, and destroy or disable those targets with 500-pound bombs and Hellfire missiles."[34] The name Reaper was obviously chosen to connote death, and US generals have referred to it as a hunter-killer weapons system.[35]

Although they are touted as precision systems, drones are responsible for numerous documented cases of "collateral damage," where innocent civilians or allies are wrongfully targeted and killed.[36] The unintended killings may be due in part to the lack of detailed intelligence or the difficulty of differentiating between combatant and civilian, but drone systems may also lend themselves to dangerous presumptions of omniscience and quick action. "'It's like a video game,' says one analyst who served at U.S. Central Command headquarters in Camp As Sayliyah in Qatar. 'It can get a little bloodthirsty. But it's fucking cool.'"[37] Unlike a video game, however, there are very real, violent results from the actions of drone pilots.

The pilots aren't immune to psychological effects, either. "You do stick around and see the aftermath of what you did, and that does personalize the fight," explains one drone operator. "You have a pretty good optical picture of the individuals on the ground. The images can be pretty graphic, pretty vivid."[38] Drone pilots who have formerly flown F-16 fighter jets say they experience a lot more emotional affect piloting UAVs because, as one pilot puts it, "I feel more connected with

FIGURE 6.1. Heron drone. Photograph from Luis Romero/Associated Press.

the ground fight than I ever did when I was flying over the top [in an F-16] at 20,000 feet."[39] Although they might be able to sleep at home at night, drone pilots can suffer psychological trauma, and the military is now offering psychiatric treatment and psychological and spiritual counseling to help them cope with it.[40]

Open Signals

In 2009 it was discovered that Iraqi insurgents had been monitoring unencrypted video footage from US Predator drones. The signals were intercepted using "$26 off-the-shelf software" and saved to the hard drives of laptop computers.[41] Evidently US personnel assumed the enemy wouldn't have this basic level of technological sophistication. Hubris is a remarkable thing. And sometimes a very effective way of resisting surveillance is to co-opt it.

Drones are also being used to patrol US borders with Mexico and Canada, as a component of the virtual fence project discussed above. In 2006 the United States spent $100 million on UAVs, and by 2010 it was operating six unarmed Predator drones along the United States–

Mexico border and testing drones along the United States–Canada border.[42] Just as the deployment of drones has increased in war zones in recent years, so too have they become a staple of border security. Thus, in 2010 President Obama "signed legislation to spend $600 million on two more unmanned drones to patrol the border and on 1,500 additional Border Patrol agents and other law-enforcement personnel to crack down on illegal immigrants and drug traffickers."[43]

Even local police departments are now using drones. According to a 2006 report, "One North Carolina county is using a UAV equipped with low-light and infrared cameras to keep watch on its citizens. The aircraft has been dispatched to monitor gatherings of motorcycle riders at the Gaston County fairgrounds from just a few hundred feet in the air—close enough to identify faces."[44] The Houston and Las Vegas Police Departments have also tested drones to assist with investigations and monitor special events.[45] And in Merseyside, UK, the police are using small helicopter drones to investigate not-so-threatening crimes like antisocial behavior and public disorder.[46]

The increase in drone surveillance raises a number of important questions. Is it ethical to use these systems to kill others, particularly when drones seem prone to collateral damage? Do we really want silent, almost invisible technologies of war hovering over our cities, scrutinizing our every move? Will they be used in prejudicial ways to monitor activists or others engaged in lawful activities? How safe are they from an aviation perspective? Will they cause airplane crashes or fall into our homes or playgrounds when they malfunction? As with most surveillance systems, questions of this sort are not currently a part of mainstream public discourse, but they absolutely should be.

Video Surveillance: The Technology of Choice

A lot of people associate the word *surveillance* with video cameras mounted on buildings or poles. While a primary goal of this book is to show the diversity and ubiquity of new technologies of surveillance in everyday life, the good old video camera is still widely used and remains a potent symbol. Video camera systems have also undergone some amazing transformations recently, so it's high time we talked about them.

There are tens of millions of video cameras—also known as closed-circuit television (CCTV) cameras—spread around the world. The

United Kingdom was early to this party, responding in part to London bomb attacks by the Irish Republican Army in 1993 and 1994 and to the horrific killing of two-year-old Jamie Bulger in 1993, where video cameras recorded the little boy being led away by his two ten-year-old assailants.[47] Thanks to generous government investments, by 2006 there were an estimated 4.2 million cameras throughout Britain—one for every fourteen people.[48]

Nowadays China is the clear leader, with 10 million cameras installed throughout the country.[49] The industrial city of Shenzhen, which churns out most of the consumer products in the world today, alone had over 200,000 surveillance cameras in 2008 and a projected 2 million by 2011.[50] Shanghai also boasts 50,000 cameras and is planning to double that figure by 2016.[51] These efforts are part of strategies by the Chinese government to implement a massive Golden Shield surveillance system that integrates video feeds, Internet use, phone tracking, voice recognition systems, RFID-embedded identification cards, and facial recognition technology, ostensibly for crime control. According to journalist Naomi Klein, "When Golden Shield is finished, there will be a photo in those databases for every person in China: 1.3 billion faces."[52]

The primary uses of these integrated security systems in China appear to be overt censorship, political repression, and religious persecution. The country is notorious for filtering Internet content about democracy, Tibet, or religion—behind the "Great Firewall"—and all Internet cafés are required to monitor their patrons with CCTV cameras linked directly to local police stations.[53] Since the violent crackdowns on pro-democracy activists at Tiananmen Square in 1989, it's been illegal for US companies to sell crime-control equipment to China. But the $33 billion market for security systems in China is simply too lucrative for US companies to pass up, so Honeywell, IBM, General Electric, and others have been ignoring this legal prohibition (or exploiting loopholes) with impunity.[54] When there were protests in Tibet leading up to the 2008 Olympic Games in Beijing, the systems were used to shut down the Internet, block phone calls and text messages, direct the police toward organizers, and generate media propaganda.[55]

Indeed, "mega-events" like the Olympic Games or the World Cup have been repeatedly harnessed by governments and industry to roll out advanced surveillance systems with minimal opposition and at great public cost.[56] The 2004 Olympic Games in Greece, for instance, saddled the country with a $15 billion bill, of which $1.5 billion was for an elaborate security system of cameras, blimps, helicopters, boats, and keyword phone-tracking systems—not to mention the seventy thousand military and security personnel, many of them armed.[57] After the festivities are over, many of the security systems remain in place and continue to be used to police the public, sometimes transforming previously open spaces into highly fortified and surveilled ones. In essence, mega-events have become a Trojan horse for radically securitizing cities and crushing governments with debt, while the global security industry gains handsomely.[58] This pattern has been reproduced, and often amplified, wherever such events are held. The 2008 Olympics in Beijing, for instance, racked up an estimated total cost of $44 billion, with $6.5 billion going to security, which included 1 million video cameras in Beijing.[59]

But It Works, Right?

Not really. While it might help police target individuals, studies show that video surveillance doesn't deter violent crime, probably because such crimes are usually spontaneous, not premeditated.[60] So CCTV doesn't increase safety, and it might make people less safe if they see cameras and (wrongly) presume that someone is watching and will rush to their aid if they're in need. Most cameras aren't monitored in real time, so that's not going to happen. CCTV does appear to reduce—or displace—some property crimes, and it can be useful in prosecuting criminals after the fact. But all things considered, simply improving street lighting has proved much more effective at reducing crime. This may change as the video surveillance systems develop.

A growing trend is toward integrating CCTV with other surveillance systems, augmenting and extending their reach well beyond the two-dimensional visual realm. With generous funding from the Department of Homeland Security, cities like Chicago have deployed a "smart surveillance" system of ten thousand public and private video cameras, which can be monitored from a centralized control room at the city's police department or from mobile units driving around the city. The cameras aren't just on the street; they include cameras in schools, public housing, and other indoor locations. Many of the police cameras are easy to spot because they're encased in white protective boxes with a conspicuous police logo and a blue light on top. What is not as obvious is that some of the camera units can also record sound (and in England some "shouting cameras" can broadcast sound: "Throw your trash in the bin!"). Additionally, as part of Chicago's Operation Virtual Shield, the cameras are just one component of a larger counterterrorism infrastructure that includes sensors throughout the city for detecting chemical and biological agents.[61]

Eyes on the Road

A few years back, the big excitement was about police cruiser cameras that could read license plates and initiate computer checks for wanted vehicles, red-light cameras that could automatically cite drivers going through intersections too late on the yellow, and speed cameras that could automatically ticket lead-footed drivers. But now it all comes together in one big package: "New camera and computer interface technologies being installed on European highways can identify several violations at once and issue automatic citations. A quick check of speed and distance between vehicles covers laws against speeding and tailgating. A quick check on the license plate numbers covers registration, insurance, and pending warrants. A quick glance inside makes sure that everyone has his or her seat belt securely fastened."[62]

While the systems haven't yet achieved their full potential, the goal with smart surveillance is to process all the video and audio feeds with software analytics "to include such features as facial recognition, audio (i.e. gunshot) recognition, pattern analysis, event storyboarding, gait analysis, behavioral analytics and centralized case management."[63] Should the system detect a gunshot or should the 911 dispatcher receive a call, the cameras will automatically pan toward the suspected location and send their video feeds to police personnel en route to the scene.[64] With gait and pattern recognition, the systems can also be programmed to identify suspicious groupings of people and send alerts to authorities. In addition to tracking suspects or their vehicles in real time, the systems can automatically search through their history to discover previous footage of that person or vehicle.[65] It might sound like science fiction, but "smart surveillance" and "automated prediction" are upon us.

Sexist Surveillance?

If it's true that the past can provide lessons for the future, many of these developments in video surveillance will become tools of high-tech voyeurism. Some of the earliest studies of video surveillance found that control-room operators, who were almost always men, would use CCTV to follow women around, zoom in on their butts or breasts, and print "screen shots" of the women for the operators' enjoyment. Other findings were that operators disproportionately follow young people and people of color. With all the technological enhancements we've been talking about, do you think these practices will dissipate?

When video surveillance is mediated by computer algorithms, we face a host of social and technical concerns. Profiling will become easier and more likely. It will be easier to compile detailed representations of people's movements, locations, interactions, and social networks. These "data doubles" may seem authentic and true even when they are partial and flawed. And there's more. Using algorithmic technology, computer scientists have already devised a way to erase people or objects from video feeds *in real time*.[66] In other words, anyone watching the video feed, even live, will not see the element that is being erased. The implications of this "diminished reality" should be terrifying. It's possible that the software could be used to protect the identities of vulnerable populations. But it's also possible that those with the power to do so might alter footage so that people engaged in criminal acts, for instance, could simply be erased—or worse, replaced with a video image of an innocent person. A whole new kind of technological literacy will be necessary to think critically about the truth of images that can be doctored automatically, without any direct human intervention or awareness.[67]

Enter the Security Network

AT&T's room 641A was always locked, and only National Security Agency (NSA) technicians had access to it. This room, in the company's San Francisco central office, was strategically chosen for its proximity to the primary switch room where all public phone calls were routed.[68] AT&T technician Mark Klein thought something was odd about this arrangement and soon discovered that the fiber optic cables to the switch room were being split into the secret NSA room so that all domestic and international telecommunications signals could be monitored. Klein further found out that the NSA had installed a "semantic traffic analyzer" that could capture and analyze all telecommunications data, not just phone calls. In his words, "Based on my understanding of the connections and equipment at issue, it appears the NSA is capable of conducting what amounts to vacuum-cleaner surveillance of all the data crossing the internet—whether that be peoples' [*sic*] e-mail, web surfing or any other data."[69] Rather than the room's being an anomaly, it turns out that similar secret rooms were set up at other AT&T facilities as well as at many other telecommunications companies.

This story of secret government spy rooms probably won't surprise you now, but in 2003 it was a monumental development in government surveillance of citizens. The USA Patriot Act—passed a mere forty-five days after the terrorist attacks on September 11, 2001—already permitted law-enforcement agencies to subpoena information from Internet service providers, cable companies, banks, and educational institutions.[70] This law also allowed the FBI to serve "national security letters" on libraries or other organizations demanding information on patrons without needing to establish the important legal threshold of "probable cause." If you got a letter, you also got a bonus—a gag order forbidding you to tell anyone about it, even your lawyer. Jail time awaited those who talked.[71]

News that secret NSA surveillance was being conducted on citizens, in collusion with telecommunications companies, was a big deal; so big, in, fact that, at the request of the White House, the *New York Times* held the story for a year before finally publishing it in 2005—notably *after* the 2004 presidential election.[72] The NSA surveillance also violated the Foreign Intelligence Surveillance Act (FISA) of 1978. In a generous move, Congress amended FISA in 2008 to grant *retroactive* immunity to the parties involved in this illegal spying. There is little doubt that the practice of joint public-private surveillance is here to stay.

The Public-Private Partnership

For those who take comfort in the idea that your phone calls, Facebook posts, and Google searches are safely separated from the prying eyes of government agents, think again. The public-private partnership in surveillance is strong, will continue to grow, and is very well hidden from any meaningful accountability.

Department of Homeland Security "fusion centers," which we mentioned briefly in chapter 2, offer another window on to this growing public-private security network. After 9/11, it was widely recognized that obstacles to sharing data among government agencies caused a failure to connect the dots to prevent the terrorist attacks. Fusion centers were initially formed to assist with merging and analyzing disparate data to find meaningful patterns that could help with counter-terrorism or criminal investigations. Housed mostly in local and state police departments across the country, analysts in these centers operate tip hotlines; merge data from federal, state, local, and tribal agencies; and purchase data from private-sector data aggregators.

As we've seen, data aggregators possess a wealth of information on individuals (ranging from credit card purchases to entertainment preferences to demographic characteristics). The data aggregator Entersect, for example, owns detailed records on 98 percent of Americans, and it frequently passes those records on to DHS fusion centers.[73] This is a troubling development because it suggests that should law-enforcement agents want to know something about you, they can use the fusion center to circumvent legal protections that previously would have required them to get a court order to engage in surveillance. It's also a two-way street. Banks, universities, hotels, defense companies like Boeing, and even Starbucks can be interpreted as "critical infrastructure," so fusion centers can share information with them and in some instances even allow private-sector representatives to be a part of investigations.[74]

The blurring of boundaries between public- and private-sector security goes much deeper. The United States "spends some $42 billion annually on private intelligence contractors, up from $17.5 billion in 2000. That means 70 per cent of the US intelligence budget is going to private companies."[75] These numbers prove once more that the classic idea of Big Brother as epitomized by repressive, centralized state surveillance is no longer accurate. Instead, the security network described here is an amalgam of state and corporate actors, disparate databases, and often ad hoc practices. Our dominant ways of thinking about and regulating government surveillance are woefully out-of-date.

WikiLeaks: In Pursuit of Transparency

Just as law-enforcement agents are exploiting the fluid exchange of data afforded by network technologies, political activists are harnessing these new potentials to expose state practices, sometimes to the dismay of government officials. WikiLeaks offers a powerful case in point. In 2010, the WikiLeaks website published classified video footage (called "Collateral Murder") of a US helicopter strike on unarmed people in Baghdad, including two Reuters news agency reporters. Apparently the soldiers in the helicopter thought the video cameras the reporters carried were rocket-propelled grenade launchers, so they proceeded to "Light 'em all up" and laugh about it.[76] Over a dozen people were killed, including the reporters, and two children were badly injured, to which one pilot responded, "Ah damn. Oh well."[77]

WikiLeaks followed up this posting with the release of confidential "diplomatic cables" and other documents confirming what many people had long known or suspected about Operation Enduring Freedom: that drone strikes in Afghanistan and Pakistan are on the rise, that civilian deaths are covered up or not seriously investigated, that truck drivers are forced to bribe Afghan police, and that the Taliban are supported by the Pakistani intelligence and army.[78] Other potentially embarrassing leaks concerned US frustration with Saudi Arabia for permitting wealthy Saudi organizations to fund Islamic militants, including the Afghan Taliban.[79] There was even a leak about the United States' agreeing to investigate the activist anti-whaling organization Sea Shepherd on behalf of the Japanese government.[80]

The government outcry over WikiLeaks was vociferous. A chief complaint was that the cable release might endanger agents, diplomats, and informants, even though WikiLeaks initially distributed the leaked documents to reputable news organizations such as the *New York Times* and *Le Monde*, which redacted names and sent edited versions to the Obama administration for further redactions.[81] Nonetheless, the organization was hard-hit on a number of fronts: Amazon kicked the site off its servers; Visa, MasterCard, and PayPal refused to process any more donations to the organization; the website and its "mirrors" were inundated with cyber "denial of service" attacks; and the US Justice Department opened an investigation into WikiLeaks founder Julian Assange and was considering charging him with espionage, even though media releases of documents are protected as freedom of speech.[82] The suspected leaker of these files, US soldier Bradley Manning, has faced the harshest treatment, including prolonged solitary confinement that many experts say is equivalent to torture and will surely cause psychological damage.[83]

WikiLeaks reveals something profound about the nature of the surveillance society. WikiLeaks is a sort of *reverse* surveillance, which turns the powers of unwanted observation back on the state. The controversy surrounding leaked government documents illustrates that just as more and more is known about individuals, institutions are trying desperately to avoid scrutiny or transparency. Yet as long as information is digitized and the Internet remains somewhat open, secrets will probably get out eventually. As surveillance studies scholar David Murakami Wood writes, "In the case of WikiLeaks, the revelation of secret information is not a breach of anyone's personal privacy, rather it is a massively important development in our ability to hold states to account in the information age."[84] Unfortunately, there is a corresponding closure of the Internet happening, whether through China-style firewalls, Google consolidation and filtering of searches, refusals by companies (like Amazon) to host politically charged content (like WikiLeaks), or automated "digital rights management" restrictions on media.[85] Ensuring that the Internet remains open will be an ongoing political, social, and technological struggle.

Conclusion

Security is a multibillion-dollar global industry. It's been called recession-proof because governments, corporations, and individuals invest in it and purchase its products regardless of the state of the economy. While security entails clear financial costs, some of which we've discussed, our main concern here is the social costs. The trends are not comforting. Individual rights are reduced at security portals such as airports and borders. Some travelers receive preferential treatment while others are subjected to racial, ethnic, religious, or political profiling. Unmanned drones have a propensity for killing innocent people in war zones and are being deployed in cities as a new wave in civilian law enforcement. Large cities are installing "smart" video surveillance to predict crime, repress dissidents, and relentlessly track people. And information is flowing freely between public and private sectors, sometimes allowing law-enforcement agents to circumvent laws intended to protect citizens from unwarranted government spying. The social costs are indeed great. Are they worth it?

People want to be protected from harm. Violent crime and terrorism rank high on the list of things we'd all like to avoid. So it makes sense on one level that the promise of protection through surveillance would be appealing. Unfortunately, study after study shows that technological surveillance is not very good at preventing crime and is probably even less effective at preventing terrorism.[86] For example, some of the known terrorist attempts since 9/11 failed because the attackers made mechanical blunders or because bystanders intervened.[87] This was the case with Richard Reid, the "shoe bomber," who tried to light explosives in his shoes on a flight from Paris to Miami in 2001: the revamped airport screening let him through, but when his shoes failed to explode, other passengers subdued him. Similarly, in 2009 Umar Farouk Abdulmutallab was unable to detonate a bomb in his underpants on a flight from Amsterdam to Detroit; the airport screening system failed to detect the explosives, but a passenger grabbed him when he realized what was going on. Finally, in 2010 American citizen Faisal Shahzad botched his attempt to detonate a car bomb in New York City's Times Square, a place teeming with video surveillance; two street vendors told the police when they heard some popping sounds and saw smoke coming from the SUV. Shahzad was nabbed after boarding an aircraft headed to Dubai. Surveillance didn't do much to prevent these unsuccessful attacks. There may be unpublicized cases where surveillance has prevented terrorism, but since intelligence successes are frequently trumpeted by the agencies involved, it would be unusual for significant achievements to remain hidden for years.[88]

We began this chapter with some stories about people's humiliating experiences with airport security. As with most stories about surveillance-based security, there's an implied contract at the heart of the drama: we put up with it because it keeps us safe. But this framing forces the question: If it doesn't really keep us safe, why do we tolerate it? The answer is complicated. One response is that most of us don't know surveillance is largely ineffective at achieving its primary objectives. Another response might be that we know surveillance is inadequate but we're comforted by the idea that at least *something* is being done, and we hope that someday it will improve. Still another answer is that most people are compliant; they're uncomfortable with challenging authority, especially when the repercussions of speaking out can be harsh, such as nominating yourself for a more invasive search or travel delays. A final reason might be that people have an almost mystical faith in the power of technologies and find it difficult to think critically about them. (Since you've come with us this far, we know that doesn't describe you.) As with a lot of questions regarding human behavior, all these answers are true for different people at different times. And while each of these answers tells us something about our public silence, the truth is that we must talk about the technological failures and social costs if we hope to make intelligent decisions about security in our lives.

Conclusion

If we've done our job as the authors of this book and you've done your job as a reader, the world should look different than it did some 127 pages ago. In the story we've been telling, your cell phones, cards, and computers are technologies of surveillance contributing to an increasing reliance on supervision as the principal way to govern us in workplaces, schools, and society at large. Almost every business transaction, educational record, online or electronic purchase, health event, legal incident, journey, or other life activity is likely to be recorded and assessed as part of an ongoing process of watching, measuring, sorting, and controlling. Traditional boundaries of time and distance evaporate as our information enters the cloud to be accessible anytime, anywhere. Traditional distinctions between the arenas of our lives evaporate as school grades affect auto insurance prices and health affects employment prospects.

The world as we know it is going through some stunning changes. This book has been an effort to tell you about some of them and raise critical questions about their effects on our lives. A lot of our work is already done. This is, after all, the *conclusion*, not the introduction. You should be generally aware of many types of surveillance and, more important, possess a broad frame of reference that helps you spot and think about types of surveillance we haven't specifically addressed. We haven't tried to cover it all. The goal here has been to use a limited set of examples that are a regular part of the typical reader's everyday life.

Like all of us, you come to this book with two overlapping but somewhat different personalities: the citizen and the intellectual. For the citizen in you, we've tried to include helpful hints, suggest strategies, or at the very least give you a heads-up about what's going on so you can more effectively manage your life.[1] As we've done this, we've also been raising lots of questions for the intellectual in you—ideas about the best ways to think about surveillance, power, and the new social realities of the surveillance society. Let's get back to those questions.

The Ten Big Ideas

At the beginning of the book we laid out a list of Ten Big Ideas. As we moved through the chapters, the big ideas were always there while we explored the details of a specific area, but they probably got lost in the action. So in the next few pages we'll revisit the list and offer some closing observations on each item. We're not going to try to get in a final word on any of these topics—the surveillance society is simply too complex and dynamic for that. Here we'll try to recap what we've seen, clarify the questions and challenges, then point you to other writers whose work can add to the introduction we've offered here.

1. Big Brother and the Right to Privacy

- The established vocabulary and entrenched ideas like privacy and Big Brother can't do justice to our new and complex situation.

Big Brother and the right to privacy are the rock stars of the prevailing vocabulary that many people use to talk about surveillance. We should start by admitting that concepts like these are meaningful parts of our cultural system that can help us visualize and discuss some aspects of the surveillance society. Orwell's Big Brother reminds us of the danger of totalizing state power and the often subtle interplay of tyranny and "concern" in surveillance regimes. The right to privacy gives voice to the vital human desire to be left alone. It ranges from having space to use the bathroom, to keeping others away from your purse, wallet, or in-box, to browsing the Internet without having others see where you've gone.[2] Both these concepts are powerful tools for depicting and summarizing critical parts of life in the surveillance society, but many of us who study surveillance full-time have concluded that they're too limiting and dated to serve as the dominant terms for our discussion.

Here's another concept that's outdated and overused: the panopticon. As we explained in chapter 1, the image of Big Brother has been joined by the idea of the panopticon, with its gentler technocratic gaze replacing the hard stare of Big Brother's telescreens. Lately there's been a recognition that the model of the panopticon doesn't capture a lot of what's going on in the surveillance society, partly because the panopticon is too fixed on the idea of one central observer watching a prisoner held in an isolated cell. But the panopticon also presumes that everyone is exposed to similar forms of observation that will transform them into well-behaved, self-governing people. This simply isn't a good representation of our experience.

As you know from this book, contemporary surveillance works by sorting people into categories and treating them differently, not all the same. And the surveillance society has millions of observers and observed spread across space and time. We're not trapped like prisoners in cells. We have many dimensions to our lives, and accordingly the powers of surveillance follow us and depict us in many different ways. Some have argued that a better way to imagine the power of surveillance is through the idea of a surveillant assemblage, which acts like a rhizome—a dense, living, weblike system of plant roots that extend underground with countless hidden nodes and visible growth shoots.[3] This metaphor may do a better job of capturing the pervasive, unpredictable, growing nature of modern surveillance.

Similar patterns are under way as intellectuals and attorneys attempt to use the idea of privacy to talk about the offenses and problems of surveillance. It's sometimes perceived as the right to be left alone, in isolation, other times as a right to control information about oneself, other times as a social value referring to the autonomy of groups, families, and individuals. Obviously, privacy has great relevance in our conversations about surveillance, and privacy will definitely be of ongoing importance in legal and political struggles over surveillance practices (more on this soon). But an increasing number of surveillance scholars are moving away from framing their work within what might be called the privacy paradigm. We're not saying we don't value privacy. We're not saying we don't support those activists and attorneys who struggle to protect our privacy. And we're not saying privacy is irrelevant to explaining the challenges of surveillance. We are saying that the privacy paradigm or the privacy regime must give way (like Big Brother, Inc.) to a more flexible, diverse, and refreshable understanding of the dynamics of power and surveillance today.

In answer to the broader question of what to call it, we urge you to resist the tendency to settle on one fixed vocabulary. All the terms have their uses, applications, and moments of relevance, and new ones are certainly needed as we confront unprecedented realities. But here's the deal: "surveillance" is so central to so many dimensions of our lives that it really takes on a wide and shifting variety of characteristics. The surveillance that picks out our movies is not the same as the surveillance that taps our phones. Work to avoid simplifying terms. The real intellectual danger is falling prey to the terminology we've inherited rather than keeping our minds and ears open to new, more effective ways to express ourselves and talk about the things that concern us.

2. The Joy of Surveillance

· Surveillance doesn't always come out of the dark recesses of Big Brother's evil scheming—at first glance, some types of surveillance look like fun and don't seem to threaten values like liberty, equality, or democratic governance.

A lot of the past writing about surveillance (including some of our own) is really gloomy. The emphasis tends to be on power, domination, the decline of privacy, and the loss of freedom. These real concerns have been a central part of this book. But let's face it: there's a lighter side to surveillance. When websites monitor you, they can also suggest new media you might enjoy. If you've got a smartphone or an up-to-date GPS in the car, you can scout ahead for a decent restaurant or local attractions in a town you've never been to. That's helpful stuff. There are even signs that surveillance can sometimes empower people who would otherwise be overlooked—think about the future scientist in a tiny town who gets discovered only because of her amazing SAT score, or the police brutality case that moves forward only because of video footage shot on a cell phone. At several points along the way, we've taken note of these helpful, playful, or harmless dimensions of new information technologies. We've presented them a bit hesitantly, because we think that, while that side of them is absolutely true, they can be misleading as representations of surveillance. Well, not misleading—confusing. Yet with something this complicated, confusion is probably good. Let us explain.

Surveillance is about power. And it's necessarily about power that's imbalanced. Those hikers were found because the authorities knew where they were; Netflix found the movie because it controls the database and the algorithms; Facebook can recommend friends because it amasses data and analyzes them as a tightly controlled and very profitable corporate enterprise; Zappos can make a good guess at what shoes you like because it's studying your habits and comparing your data with information on all sorts of other people. Do *you* have access to the databases they use? Do you understand the algorithms they apply? Could you drop into a meeting and change policy? Did you even read the user agreement, privacy policy, and legal waivers you signed to get access? Very few people can answer yes to any of these questions.

This simple reality check reminds us about the imbalance of power and access built into systems of surveillance. As we've seen several times in this book, surveillance is about watching from above; it's an expression of visual and communicative power that's intended to change behavior and affect social outcomes. It's not just looking around. We've made a point of including stories about the nonthreatening side of surveillance because that's the true telling of the complexity that characterizes our lives. But within that complexity is an overall tendency that undeniably marks surveillance programs as anti-democratic expressions of concentrated power and control.

When we fully confront the contexts of anti-democratic power and control that we face in our daily lives, we're forced to ask exceptionally difficult questions about the nature of our social and political world. We may be a "democracy" to the extent that some of us vote every twenty-four or forty-eight months and some might sign petitions or donate to organizations that lobby for our causes in Washington. But when you think of our daily lives, with hours logged at workplaces and schools defined by surveillance and control and "free time" frequently dominated by participation in highly organized, corporate-sponsored recreation and amusements, the image of democratic living begins to break down. When surveillance characterizes almost all aspects of social life but most surveillance is undemocratic, then we are clearly moving toward a less democratic society. The many enjoyable moments of surveillance may be accustoming us to life in the surveillance society and making it difficult for us to think critically about it.

3. The Public-Private Partnership

- Picturing "big government" as the principal source of modern surveillance is wrong. Governments are important players, but most of the innovative new surveillance initiatives are coming from the corporate sector, which frequently links up with governments in a contractual relationship.

Google, Facebook, Verizon, AT&T, Comcast, Raytheon, Boeing, Amazon, ChoicePoint, Entersect, LexisNexis, and more—these are the labs leading the Research and Development Department of the surveillance society. The corporate sector has more talent, more money, and more legal autonomy than the government and has forged the cutting edge in designing and using new technological systems. Along with the not-too-shabby programs in the national defense agencies, this group forms a rich and diverse array of institutions engaged in a largely uncoordinated campaign of massive surveillance.

This has obvious implications for how we think about the nature of governance and the challenges that face us as citizens, consumers, and employees. We all too frequently consider government the primary threat to freedom and autonomy, but that's no longer true. The fusion of government and corporate power is so clear and so strong that we really need to reimagine how we think about our political society if we hope to transcend the inherited tendency to see the world as having a public sector and a private sector. What we face is a more diffuse set of challenges in which public- and private-sector powers align in a broad push for ever more information about all dimensions of our lives.

In this book we've seen the reality of these practices when phone companies give the National Security Agency special access to their wires, when cell phone carriers help law enforcement locate individuals, when Yahoo! cooperates with Chinese authorities trying to round up activists, and when schools contract with for-profit companies for their testing and security services. Less obviously, since we've argued that surveillance pervades society, public and private sectors logically cooperate to advance a state of permanent visibility of individual actions and transactions. So even if your bank is not, for the moment, actively reporting your credit card activity to the government, every transaction is recorded so it can be reported and analyzed at any time in the future. This makes your bank a very effective and important agency in generating personal visibility. If you accept our claim that compelled visibility is a central means of governance in the surveillance society, then the many institutions that compel visibility are implicated in the emergent regime.

4. Making New Worlds

· Surveillance does more than just watch. Surveillance also *shapes* our "selves" by creating odd edited versions of who we are (a test score, a driving record, a credit risk) to form the basis for decisions about us. And surveillance also *makes* our world by establishing patterns of reward and punishment that guide our choices and behaviors.

There are two senses in which surveillance "makes" the world. First, it distills complex and changing situations into stable and usable images. Even the humble snapshot "makes" a world in that it eliminates anything outside the viewfinder or beyond the camera's range and leaves off the stories of what came before and after the picture was taken. The massive gatherings of data and information we've seen in this book are really just more complicated versions of the same process. A presentation of someone's data may include things like credit scores, legal activities, shopping preferences, wealth, and tax statements, but it can never be close to a complete and true telling of a human life. Some aspects of our lives are emphasized while others are excluded. We go through countless recombinations as we are "remade" for different organizational purposes. So surveillance makes us and our world by constructing the images that then define us.

Surveillance also makes the world in the sense that human behavior changes in response to surveillance. School curricula change in the face of mandatory testing; doctors and nurses change their treatment of patients under new patient-tracking protocols; drivers adjust their speed when they detect police radar. These examples deliver the lesson that surveillance is not just watching the world: it constructs the world, shapes behavior, and instills values. And though we're giving a lot of agency to the various forms of surveillance out there, it bears remembering that there are always people behind such systems. Even automated Google algorithms or keystroke-tracking programs in the workplace had to be programmed and implemented by someone.

This recognition of its creative powers makes our effort to understand surveillance a lot harder (and more interesting). That's because most popular stories about surveillance assume that it's a system of watching, not a system of world making. If we're "made" by surveillance, what does it do to us, as citizens and consumers, to exist in multiple forms, in multiple places and times, fulfilling the multiple needs of institutions? How can any idea of a central or fixed public version of our "selves" persist in such a context? And what do we learn about our social lives and societal futures as we begin to understand that each act of surveillance is not just an observation, but also a creative value-laden act launching new behavioral codes and ideals? Instead of just worrying about who might be watching and why, the deeper concern should be about what kind of world is being created.

5. Fear and Desire in the Surveillance Society

- It is incomplete to think of surveillance *only* as something forced on an unwilling populace. Many people sign up for, support, and participate in surveillance programs. The twin forces of fear and desire are central to understanding why we so often love surveillance.

Fear and desire catalyze many of the advances in surveillance that we've covered in this book. We respond to our fears as we beef up borders, airport checkpoints, school and home security systems, and the like. We respond to desire when we *must* have the latest new phone, app, or credit card. Before we get into specific examples, remember that fear and desire work closely together. A desire to stay tethered to Facebook can grow out of the fear of being socially excluded. And a desire to live in a gated community with security patrols can emerge from the fear of vulnerability.

You won't be at all surprised to hear that campaigns to raise our desires are prolific—that's what advertising is all about. It teaches us to need and want perfect skin, a new president, a new iProduct. We're used to that. But it's critical to note that there's something akin to ad campaigns on the fear side too. Intensifications of surveillance frequently accompany a sense of crisis. Notice we didn't say intensifications of surveillance "are caused by crises" or "emerge in response to crises." That's because we think the whole question of causation is often highly suspect.

Surveillance thrives on an abundance of crises. Will it be illegal immigration? Or the threat of a terrorist attack? Or child abductions? Or teen drug use? Or the national debt? Or unemployment? Or runaway executive salaries and corporate earnings? Or the lack of quality health care for millions? You get the idea. Social crises and public problems do not get our attention on their own; media and politics influence the process. There's almost always a good crisis or frightening threat to run with.[4] Communists. Urban gangs. Terrorists. Crackheads. Pedophiles. Illegal immigrants. Guns in schools. Druggies in the workplace. Identity theft. Eek! Somebody do something!

As you know all too well, the political-media spin cycle is able to freak out over problems whether they're real or imagined. The cycles are fed by rotating combinations of actual social problems, media outlets looking for hype, politicians looking for attention, government agencies looking for budget lines, a population looking for scary amusements, and industries looking for contracts. And there's almost always some new surveillance available to respond to the crisis. It could be full-body scanners at airports, credit-monitoring services for identity theft, RFID badges for students, drug tests for workers, facial recognition video cameras on city streets, or unmanned drones patrolling the border.

A few pages back, we argued that living in surveillance societies breeds an expectation that someone will be watching us. A counterpart is that we also come to hope someone is watching out *for* us. It's a scary world out there. When we walk in fear, we not only don't resent the surveillance that increasingly pervades our lives; we appreciate it. Particular moments of crisis augment and focus our fear and legitimate new mechanisms and practices of surveillance. There are a host of new technologies in development at any given time—they're demonstrated at security trade shows and pushed in professional magazines and conventions. When the next big crisis comes along, some company will be ready with the amazing new technological fix that will make us feel safe again.

Many people also want to be watched so they can feel like they're a part of something. People post to Facebook and respond to others to create community; they want others to engage with them. Authors like us want people to read what we write, and we hope readers appreciate what we're trying to do. Millions of people on cell phones don't appear to be talking about anything too pressing, but instead of just waiting until they get home to call or e-mail, they banter and text while shopping, driving, or walking—some don't even hang up when they're peeing! For better or worse, this desire to be watched, read, or heard is a fundamental element in the evolution of the surveillance society. It drives us toward voluntary disclosure and desensitizes us to outside scrutiny.

6. Now Appearing in 4-D!

· Surveillance challenges the ways we typically think about space and time.

At first glance, the stories are simple. A college party generates some wild pictures that are posted on the web. A crazy weekend fling is fueled by a cluster of credit card charges in bars, strip joints, and bail-bond offices. An automobile accident is recorded in the insurance industry data set. So be it. Life goes on. But then, years later, these stories reappear in the life of someone who is no longer a carefree twenty-year-old; in attempting to get a job, a security clearance, or some other privileged access, the past is no longer the past. The past is now present.

We don't need to be fans of science fiction to note that the future can also, in a sense, become the present, because many elements of surveillance have to do with predicting behavior. SATs, ACTs, GREs, and LSATs, for example, are all efforts to predict your performance in college or graduate school. Your insurance ratings predict your driving record, your health, and your likely age of death. You'll be billed accordingly. Neither your college, your law school, nor your insurance company wants to face a rude awakening, so they're all going to do everything they can to predict and plan for the future, with significant implications for the present.

Just as surveillance blurs traditional understandings of time, surveillance technologies frequently challenge our understanding of space. As I'm writing these words, my coauthor is about five hundred miles away, but thanks to the cloud computing software Dropbox, every time I hit Save he gets a little flash in the upper right-hand corner of his computer screen. This visibility signals to him that I'm hard at work (or not) and effectively transports him to my office as a nonpresent observer. You can recall other stories of our geographic meltdown: a drone in Iraq is piloted by a guy in California; a runaway Ohio girl driving down an Arkansas highway is pinpointed by cell phone signals captured by satellite and analyzed somewhere else; children from all over the world are placed on one international grid of standardized test results. It's a small world after all. And it's getting smaller all the time.

7. Resisting the Gaze

- There may be a massive uncelebrated anti-surveillance movement formed by all the people who cheat, lie, evade, trick, or otherwise undermine surveillance programs.

Millions of people use fake ID cards; millions take steps to enhance their test scores; millions fill out their tax returns in creative ways; millions illegally download and share music, movies, and software; millions engage in black-market activities hidden from the government. All these people and all this activity can't simply be written off as cheating. In the world of surveillance, it's far more important and interesting than that. We've argued that these are practices of everyday resistance: little ways that relatively powerless people can use petty rule-breaking, evasion, or fibbing to get away with something. Since these actions can limit the power of surveillance *and* challenge the system's demand that we always tell the whole truth, they're a significant form of politics in the surveillance society.[5]

But we need to be careful about one possible misunderstanding. We're not making the argument that everyday resistance can somehow replace more fundamental challenges to existing patterns of power in the surveillance society. Everyday resistance is not a substitute for this type of political action. Getting away with an unscheduled nap at work is not a bold and effective way to "stick it to the man." Cheating on your taxes will not precipitate the decline and fall of the surveillance society. And resistance often invites further, even more intensive surveillance as authorities from the IRS or the insurance industry or the Recording Industry Association of America try to figure out how to catch rule breakers. So we are certainly not positioning everyday resistance as a cure-all. What we're arguing here is that practices of everyday resistance are a widespread form of politics that needs to be taken seriously as we struggle to understand this new world. If our public discussions did more than simply write off all forms of resistance as cheating, and got into a more intelligent discussion about struggles for power, we'd all have a much richer understanding of politics.

Throughout this book, we've argued that you're pretty much on your own as a citizen of the surveillance society and that you need to be fully informed about the challenges you face and the tools at your disposal. Resistance is one of those tools. We've talked about the limits of government action, privacy rights, and other organized schemes that might protect us and, simply put, we're not waiting for the cavalry to come over the ridge. In short, if we were deeply concerned about our online privacy and had to pick between scrutinizing user agreements and privacy policies, writing our congressional representative, or learning how to use anonymizing software, we'd both pick the software. Hands down. Every time.

But you might want to make a different or an additional choice. At several points in this book, we've talked about organizations and activities tied to the international privacy movement—groups like the Electronic Privacy Information Center, the American Civil Liberties Union, Privacy International, Statewatch, the Privacy Rights Clearinghouse, and the Electronic Frontier Foundation. These organizations unite citizens, attorneys, technologists, and scholars in a movement working to protect the rights of individuals and limit and regulate many types of surveillance. They are some of the best resources for more information and perspective on the issues discussed in this book and for opportunities to get formally involved with the politics of surveillance. (You can find links to their web pages in the Further Explorations section at the end of the book.)

8. Inequality in the Surveillance Society

- Systems of surveillance are often unique new expressions of power, but they join existing social patterns tied to inequalities of race, class, and gender.

Throughout this book we've seen classic patterns of racism emerge in even the most innovative forms of surveillance. We've seen how CCTV surveillance systems track minority youth; how people of color are overselected for airport pat-downs; how standardized tests reflect and cement existing race and class inequities; and so on. There are certainly some applications in which technocratic forms of surveillance help us become *more* color-blind—red-light cameras don't sort by the race of the driver, as police officers too frequently do—but there appears to be a general tendency for *the forms* of power expressed through surveillance to reflect and advance existing patterns of inequality and discrimination.

This shouldn't shock us when we remind ourselves that a lot of surveillance involves institutions and authorities watching and controlling people who have less power or fewer resources. Given that the imbalances of power tilt in favor of the wealthy, white, and well-connected, surveillance systems in which the more powerful watch the less powerful will necessarily reflect those broader patterns. Complicating the picture, however, affluent people are frequently subject to different types of systematic observation: for example, at airports, in the banking industry, or in online commerce. These folks may be relatively insulated from surveillance by roving squad cars and the expanding penal system that stands behind them, but they can be more exposed to gentler types of surveillance.

A vivid and troubling lesson we can take from examining the practices of surveillance in schools, workplaces, and communities is that those lower on the socioeconomic ladder face denser, meaner, and more consequential surveillance than their richer and, typically, whiter fellow citizens. Schools for rich kids have an amiable assistant principal, while schools for poor kids have armed police officers. Applicants for blue-collar jobs have to pee in a cup, while applicants for white-collar jobs might get a discreet background check. Gated communities have armed patrols protecting them from outsiders, while low-income communities are patrolled by armed outsiders. These are all forms of surveillance. But they are very different forms of surveillance. And those differences turn on the long-standing fault lines of race and class.

9. A Lot of Surveillance Simply Doesn't Work

- As pervasive and impressive as surveillance systems are, they don't always work. Or, more accurately, they don't always produce the desired or promised results.

Why do we do it? Drug tests might identify marijuana users but miss the alcoholics and speed freaks. Removing our shoes at the airport responds to one failed bombing attempt a few years back but misses a host of other threats. Remote-control spy cams on student computers may not prevent a lot of thefts, but they allow school authorities to monitor the lives of their students. Behind the technocratic authority and scientifically framed policies, surveillance systems will always be flawed attempts to observe and control social behaviors. And social behaviors will always prove too complex and mutable to be accurately represented or effectively controlled. And yet we continue. Errors in problem identification, limits to technological capacity, media-induced panic responses, entrepreneurial opportunism, and our seemingly insatiable desire for a grand high-tech fix to our problems each plague and misguide surveillance initiatives.

A lot of the trouble here is created by industry advertising and government agencies that aggressively promise too much from surveillance programs. Elsewhere in this chapter, we talk about the crisis-panic-response cycle that repeatedly plays out in the world of mass-mediated politics. And so, for example, tragic but infrequent instances of terrorism lead to spending billions of dollars on high-tech security systems. We can never know how many attacks, if any, have been prevented, but by all accounts, terrorist attacks remain incredibly rare. What we can know is that billions that might have been spent on social programs or other needs have gone to security systems, intelligence agencies, and private contractors.

The sometimes utterly irrational way we adopt new technologies can often lead people to think that technological innovation has a life of its own—that almost any new machine or technology will be pursued whether or not it makes sense. We don't think this argument will fly, because a lot of inventions never leave the shop. But it also won't fly because there are always human beings responsible for the choices made. Some of these choices may be dumb and regrettable, but they are choices nonetheless. In the current age, the people who have the power to make choices about surveillance technologies are tending very strongly toward a total commitment to the idea that more information is always better. This translates into more surveillance is always better. Why? Read on.

10. Can't Help Myself

· Scientific rationalism is the dominant mentality of our time, leading to an insatiable hunger for information. Because of this, organizations are almost always pro-surveillance.

You may have noticed we're particularly interested in what might be called do-it-yourself strategies for coping with life in the surveillance society: avoidance tactics, everyday resistance, anonymizing software, prepaid cell phones, cash, and other simple, independent tactics you can use in your daily life. You may have also noticed that even though we've argued that most surveillance cultivates an anti-democratic organization of power that threatens human freedom, we don't have a section explaining how we can all unite and take action to stop the spread of surveillance. Our editor would really like some sort of upbeat call to action as we approach the end of the book, but he's going to be disappointed. That's because, alas, it would probably be wishful thinking.

The surveillance society is sponsored by a combination of powerful industries and the massive system of modern government. It's pushed along by cyclical crises, technological momentum, and an array of ideological supports. For meaningful and potentially effective opposition to emerge, this currently unbeatable assembly of forces would have to experience some major fracture or realignment.

Today's organizations both require and create orderly, systematic knowledge about the people and things they govern or manage. Surveillance is in the DNA of the modern organization. Businesses, governments, universities, even individuals, seek to gather and organize information as an ongoing part of their work. It's simply part of what we're expected to do as responsible actors. Think about how many of our contemporary ideologies or value systems celebrate unfettered access to information. Science must have its data. Law must have its witnesses and confessions. Religion has its all-knowing deities. Democracy has its transparency. Rationality must have its perfect information. They all want to know more! This is a unique cultural alignment in which our key value systems unite to push us toward the celebration and advancement of surveillance as a means of social organization and control. In the face of this level of government, corporate, and ideological convergence in favor of advancing surveillance, we are skeptical that the flood can be pushed back. But we might be able to make it a bit more fair, transparent, and accountable. That's why we wrote this book: to help our students, our friends, and our readers figure out how to make sense of—and hopefully change—the world we share.

NOTES

Introduction

1. There are multiple surveillance societies, and multiple dimensions of surveillance in any one society. As David Murakami Wood has argued, cultural differences greatly influence the form, meaning, and practices of surveillance taking place, so the surveillance society in one country may be significantly different from the surveillance society in another. While it is more accurate to think of this in the plural as "surveillance societies," we employ the singular to stress what we see as common trends or possibilities across surveillance societies. See David Murakami Wood, "The 'Surveillance Society': Questions of History, Place and Culture," *European Journal of Criminology* 6, no. 2 (2009): 179–94.
2. Board of Governors of the Federal Reserve System, "Report to the Congress on Credit Scoring and Its Effects on the Availability and Affordability of Credit," August 2007, accessed August 20, 2011, http://www.federalreserve.gov/boarddocs/ rptcongress/creditscore/creditscore.pdf.
3. A great introduction can be found online in a special series of articles in the journal *Surveillance & Society*: http://www.surveillance-and-society.org/ojs/index.php/ journal/article/downloadSuppFile/privacy_defence/privacy_debate, accessed August 17, 2011.
4. Because surveillance is ubiquitous, we're necessarily going to miss some critical installations. Two of the most obvious examples are life in the military and life in the penal complex of prison, probation, and parole. There are over 2 million Americans on active or reserve duty in the military and more than 7 million caught up in the penal system—that's a lot of people and a lot of surveillance, but for this book we've chosen to omit those arenas while still discussing general issues of social inequality with other examples.

Chapter One

1. ITU News, "The World in 2010: ICT Facts and Figures," *ITU News*, December 2010, accessed June 30, 2011, http://www.itu.int/net/itunews/issues/2010/10/04 .aspx; CTIA, "Wireless Quick Facts: Year End Figures," *CTIA.org*, December

2010, accessed June 30, 2011, http://www.ctia.org/advocacy/research/index.cfm/aid/10323.

2. Aden Hepburn, "Statistics: The Growth of Mobile into 2011," *Digital Buzz*, November 21, 2010, accessed June 30, 2011, http://www.digitalbuzzblog.com/mobile-statistics-2011-growth-of-mobile.

3. "Triangulation" simply means that by having directional cell phone readings from more than one site, you can map a zone from each site to locate the phone at the point where the zones cross. Signal-strength data narrow the range even more. That's why more antennae give a closer read. These data are logged by cell service providers and can be used to reconstruct the location of any phone.

4. Eli Lake, "Fed Contractor, Cell Phone Maker Sold Spy System to Iran," *Washington Times*, April 13, 2009, accessed June 30, 2011, http://www.washingtontimes.com/news/2009/apr/13/europe39s-telecoms-aid-with-spy-tech; Christopher Rhoads and Loretta Chao, "Iran's Web Spying Aided by Western Technology," *Wall Street Journal*, June 22, 2009, accessed June 30, 2011, http://online.wsj.com/article/SB124562668777335653.html.

5. American Islamic Congress, "Boycott Nokia for Iran Crackdown," *American Islamic Congress*, April 21, 2009, accessed June 30, 2011, http://campaigns.aicongress.org/?id=nokia.

6. Michael Curry, David J. Phillips, and Priscilla M. Regan, "Emergency Response Systems and the Creeping Legibility of People and Places," *Information Society* 20 (2004): 357–69.

7. The stated price for each "ping" of a cell phone's GPS is $150, but it's highly likely that law-enforcement agencies received some kind of "bulk discount," because there's no way they could have afforded the full cost. As Stephanie K. Pell and Christopher Soghoian explain, "Had Sprint charged $150 for each of the 8 million pings, it would have made 1.2 billion dollars. Since law enforcement certainly did not spend that much money for this purpose, some new billing arrangement must have motivated the increased activity level" (32). Stephanie K. Pell and Christopher Soghoian, "Can You See Me Now: Toward Reasonable Standards for Law Enforcement Access to Location Data That Congress Could Enact," *Social Science Research Network*, n.d., accessed July 1, 2011, http://papers.ssrn.com/sol3/papers.cfm?abstract_id=1845644; Justin Elliott, "Police Tapped Sprint Customer GPS Data 8 Million Times in a Year," *TPM*, December 4, 2009, accessed June 30, 2011, http://tpmmuckraker.talkingpointsmemo.com/2009/12/revelation_8_million_gps_searches_on_sprint_by_law.php.

8. Phone games and other interactive applications invite users to disclose information about themselves too, including locational information that can be logged by others. For instance, one such application allows phone users to receive coupons for products (like McDonald's iced coffee) delivered to their phones, provided they register online and divulge geographic and personal information.

9. Michael Liedtke, "Know Where Your Kids Are? Check Google Maps," *MSNBC*

.com, February 4, 2009, accessed June 7, 2011, http://www.msnbc.msn.com/id/29012946.

10. Ibid.

11. Brian X. Chen, "Why and How Apple Is Collecting Your iPhone Location Data," *Wired.com*, April 21, 2011, accessed June 30, 2011, http://www.wired.com/gadgetlab/2011/04/apple-iphone-tracking.

12. Declan McCullagh, "Exclusive: Google's Web Mapping Can Track Your Phone," *CNET.com*, June 15, 2011, accessed June 30, 2011, http://news.cnet.com/8301–31921_3–20070742-281/exclusive-googles-web-mapping-can-track-your-phone.

13. John Fuller, "How Bluetooth Surveillance Works," *How Stuff Works* 2009, accessed June 7, 2011, http://electronics.howstuffworks.com/bluetooth-surveillance.htm.

14. Ibid.

15. Declan McCullagh and Anne Broache, "FBI Taps Cell Phone Mic as Eavesdropping Tool," *CNET News*, December 1, 2006, accessed June 7, 2011, http://news.cnet.com/FBI-taps-cell-phone-mic-as-eavesdropping-tool/2100–1029_3–6140191.html.

16. http://www.flexispy.com, accessed June 30, 2011.

17. Martin C. Libicki and US National Defense Research Institute, *Byting Back: Regaining Information Superiority against 21st-Century Insurgents* (Santa Monica, CA: Rand Corporation, 2007).

18. More accurately, the locational function of cell phones makes it *possible* to call for help and have it come to the right place. A strong case can be made that safety systems, including cell phones, can also instill a false sense of security, which may make people both more careless and more vulnerable.

19. Eric Wingerter, "More than 800 People Utilize NAACP Police Misconduct Rapid Reporting System," *NAACP*, January 20, 2010, accessed June 30, 2011, http://org2.democracyinaction.org/o/2446/t/9129/blog/comments.jsp?key=171&blog_entry_KEY=730&t=.

20. This interpretation corresponds with Michel Foucault's development of the concept of power and has been mobilized by other surveillance studies scholars. These insights about power apply to many, if not all, modern institutional arrangements, even if surveillance is not the primary focus. Michel Foucault, *Discipline and Punish: The Birth of the Prison* (New York: Vintage, 1977); Torin Monahan, *Surveillance in the Time of Insecurity* (New Brunswick, NJ: Rutgers University Press, 2010); Kevin D. Haggerty and Richard V. Ericson, "The Surveillant Assemblage," *British Journal of Sociology* 51, no. 4 (2000): 605–22.

21. Jackie Cohen, "ALERT: Job Screening Agency Archiving All Facebook," *All Facebook*, June 20, 2011, accessed June 30, 2011, http://www.allfacebook.com/alert-job-screening-agency-archiving-all-facebook-2011–06.

22. At a roundtable meeting with high school students, President Obama warned: "I want everybody here to be careful about what you post on Facebook, because in

the YouTube age, whatever you do, it will be pulled up again later somewhere in your life." Karen Travers, "Political Aspirations? Watch Out for Facebook, President Obama Says," *ABC News*, September 14, 2009, accessed June 30, 2011, http://abcnews.go.com/Politics/political-aspirations-watch-facebook-president-obama/story?id=8555142.

23. George Orwell, *Nineteen Eighty-Four*, centennial ed. (New York: Harcourt Brace, 1949), quotation on 64.

24. Foucault, *Discipline and Punish*.

25. David Lyon, *Surveillance as Social Sorting: Privacy, Risk, and Digital Discrimination* (New York: Routledge, 2003).

26. Haggerty and Ericson, "Surveillant Assemblage"; Torin Monahan and Tyler Wall, "Somatic Surveillance: Corporeal Control through Information Networks," *Surveillance & Society* 4, no. 3 (2007): 154–73.

27. Louis D. Brandeis and Samuel D. Warren, "The Right to Privacy," *Harvard Law Review* 4, no. 5 (1890): 193, 195–97.

28. Colin J. Bennett, *The Privacy Advocates: Resisting the Spread of Surveillance* (Cambridge, MA: MIT Press, 2008).

29. Langdon Winner, *The Whale and the Reactor: A Search for Limits in an Age of High Technology* (Chicago: University of Chicago Press, 1986).

Chapter Two

1. Connie Prater, "What You Buy, Where You Shop May Affect Your Credit," *CreditCards.com*, October 14, 2009, accessed July 19, 2011, http://www.creditcards.com/credit-card-news/how-shopping-can-affect-credit-1282.php.

2. Federal Trade Commission, "Federal Trade Commission v. CompuCredit Corporation and Jefferson Capital Systems, LLC," (2008), accessed July 19, 2011, http://www.ftc.gov/os/caselist/0623212/080610compucreditcmplt.pdf.

3. Jonathan Kent, "Malaysia Car Thieves Steal Finger," *BBC News*, March 31, 2005, accessed July 19, 2011, http://news.bbc.co.uk/2/hi/asia-pacific/4396831.stm.

4. Torin Monahan and Tyler Wall, "Somatic Surveillance: Corporeal Control through Information Networks," *Surveillance & Society* 4, no. 3 (2007): 154–73.

5. Ellen McCarthy, "Cash, Charge or Fingerprint?" *Washington Post*, June 9, 2005, accessed July 19, 2011, http://www.washingtonpost.com/wp-dyn/content/article/2005/06/08/AR2005060802335.html.

6. Green Data Systems, "Finger Vein Authentication Technology," *Green Data Systems* 2010, accessed July 19, 2011, http://www.greendatasystems.com/Hitachi-Security-Technology.html; George Webster, "Biometric ATM Gives Cash via 'Finger Vein' Scan," *CNN.com*, July 5, 2010, accessed July 19, 2011, http://articles.cnn.com/2010–07-05/world/first.biometric.atm.europe_1_banking-markets-polish-bank-bank-cards?_s=PM:WORLD; Chirasrota Jena, "Biometric ATMs for Rural India," *Express Computer*, March 12, 2007, accessed July 19, 2011, http://www.expresscomputeronline.com/20070312/technology01.shtml.

7. "Iris Recognition to Access Your Bank Account?" *Money Watch*, June 20, 2011, accessed July 7, 2011, http://money-watch.co.uk/8466/iris-recognition-to-access-your-bank-account; "Log-in to Facebook with an Iris Scan: Eye-Scanner for Your PC Set to Go on the Market in Months," *Daily Mail Reporter*, May 11, 2011, accessed July 7, 2011, http://www.dailymail.co.uk/sciencetech/article-1385959/Under-look-key-PC-iris-scanner-security-device-set-market-months.html.

8. Centers for Disease Control and Prevention, "Investigation Update: Multistate Outbreak of Human Salmonella Montevideo Infections," May 4, 2010, accessed July 19, 2011, http://www.cdc.gov/salmonella/montevideo/index.html.

9. David Mercer, "CDC Used Frequent-Shopper Cards to Find Salmonella," *USA Today*, March 10, 2010, accessed July 19, 2011, http://www.usatoday.com/money/industries/food/2010–03-10-cdc-shopper-cards-salmonella_N.htm.

10. Nils Zurawski, "Local Practice and Global Data: Loyalty Cards, Social Practices, and Consumer Surveillance," *Sociological Quarterly* 52, no. 4 (2011): 509–27.

11. The group CASPIAN (Consumers Against Supermarket Privacy Invasion and Numbering) was founded by Christian activist Katherine Albrecht, who sees radio-frequency identification (RFID) cards as possibly being "the mark of the beast" as foretold in the Bible's book of Revelation. She has started a national campaign against RFID cards in particular. Katherine Albrecht, "Auto-ID: Tracking Everything, Everywhere," *EndTime Magazine* 2003, accessed July 19, 2011, http://www.endtime.com/pdf/archives/ETM-2003-07-Autoid-Tracking-Everything.pdf. See also http://www.nocards.org, accessed July 7, 2011.

12. Finn Brunton and Helen Nissenbaum, "Vernacular Resistance to Data Collection and Analysis: A Political Theory of Obfuscation," *First Monday* 16, no. 5 (2011), accessed July 19, 2011, http://firstmonday.org/htbin/cgiwrap/bin/ojs/index.php/fm/article/view/3493/2955; Stuart Silverstein, "What Price Loyalty?" *Los Angeles Times*, February 7, 1999, accessed July 19, 2011, http://articles.latimes.com/1999/feb/07/business/fi-5738/2.

13. Erik Baard, "Buying Trouble," *Village Voice*, July 23, 2002, accessed July 19, 2011, http://www.villagevoice.com/2002-07-23/news/buying-trouble/1.

14. Robert Moran, "Eye Tracking: Interview with Barbara Barclay of Tobii," *Future of Insight*, January 8, 2011, accessed July 19, 2011, http://www.futureofinsight.com/2011/01/eye-tracking-interview-with-barbara-barclay-of-tobii.

15. Brunton and Nissenbaum, "Vernacular Resistance to Data Collection and Analysis."

16. Klever Marketing, "Competitive Advantage," 2009, accessed July 19, 2011, http://www.kleverkart.com/competitive_advantage.html.

17. Klever Marketing, "System Components," 2009, accessed July 19, 2011, http://www.kleverkart.com/system_components.html.

18. Ben Woolsey and Matt Schulz, "Credit Card Statistics, Industry Facts, Debt Statistics," *CreditCards.com*, July 14, 2011, accessed July 19, 2011, http://www.creditcards.com/credit-card-news/credit-card-industry-facts-personal-debt-statistics-1276.php.

19. Ibid.

20. Neighborhood Link, "How Landlords Can Use Credit Scoring to Make Rental Decisions," 2010, accessed July 19, 2011, http://www.neighborhoodlink.com/article/Homeowner/Credit_Scoring_Rentals.

21. Sandra Block, "Your Money: Bad Credit Can Inflate Car Insurance Premiums," *USA Today*, June 11, 2007, accessed July 19, 2011, http://www.usatoday.com/money/perfi/columnist/block/2007–06-11-ym-credit-car_N.htm.

22. Torin Monahan, *Surveillance in the Time of Insecurity* (New Brunswick, NJ: Rutgers University Press, 2010).

23. Ibid.

24. David Lyon, *Identifying Citizens: ID Cards as Surveillance* (Cambridge: Polity, 2009), 4.

25. ID Badges, "ID Card Systems Provide More than Student ID's, They Help Schools Create a Secure Learning Environment" (2011), accessed July 19, 2011, http://www.eidbadges.com/student.htm.

26. Larry Jacobs, "Hotel Guests' Eyes Serve as Room Keys," *ABC News*, July 30, 2004, accessed July 19, 2011, http://abcnews.go.com/Technology/story?id=97268&page=1.

27. National Conference of State Legislatures, "REAL ID Act of 2005: Summary," 2006, accessed July 19, 2011, http://www.ncsl.org/default.aspx?tabid=13579.

28. Center for Democracy and Technology, "PASS ID Act of 2009 Overview" (Center for Democracy and Technology, 2009), accessed July 19, 2011, http://www.cdt.org/security/20090615_PASS_ID_chart.pdf; Richard Esguerra, "PASS ID: REAL ID Reanimated" (Electronic Frontier Foundation, 2009), accessed July 19, 2011, http://www.eff.org/deeplinks/2009/08/pass-id-real-id-reanimated.

29. David Murakami Wood, "UK ID Card Program Scrapped after Election (and More)," *Notes from the Ubiquitous Surveillance Society*, May 12, 2010, accessed July 19, 2011, http://ubisurv.wordpress.com/2010/05/12/uk-id-card-program-scrapped-after-election-and-more.

30. Electronic Privacy Information Center, "REAL ID Implementation Review: Few Benefits, Staggering Costs" (2008), accessed July 19, 2011, http://epic.org/privacy/id_cards/epic_realid_0508.pdf.

31. Torin Monahan, "Identity Theft Vulnerability: Neoliberal Governance through Crime Construction," *Theoretical Criminology* 13, no. 2 (2009): 155–76.

32. Torin Monahan, "Questioning Surveillance and Security," in *Surveillance and Security: Technological Politics and Power in Everyday Life*, ed. Torin Monahan, 1–23 (New York: Routledge, 2006).

33. Stephen Baker, *The Numerati* (New York: Houghton Mifflin, 2008), 75.

34. See some examples at http://www.acxiom.com/products_and_services/background_screening/products_and_services/Pages/ProductsandServices.aspx, accessed July 19, 2011.

35. Torin Monahan, "The Future of Security? Surveillance Operations at Homeland Security Fusion Centers," *Social Justice* 37, no. 2–3 (2011): 84–98; Robert O'Harrow

Jr., "Centers Tap into Personal Databases; State Groups Were Formed after 9/11," *Washington Post*, April 2, 2008.

36. InfraGard, "Become a Member of InfraGard," 2010, accessed June 23, 2010, http://www.infragard.net/member.php.

37. Michael German and Jay Stanley, "What's Wrong with Fusion Centers?" December 2007, http://www.aclu.org/files/pdfs/privacy/fusioncenter_20071212.pdf.

Chapter Three

1. "Visualizing Everything Facebook Knows about You," *Information Aesthetics*, December 8, 2011, accessed December 27, 2011, http://infosthetics.com/archives/2011/12/all_the_information_facebook_knows_about_you.html.

2. Michael Barbaro and Tom Zeller, "A Face Is Exposed for AOL Searcher No. 4417749," *New York Times*, August 9, 2006, accessed June 17, 2011, http://www.nytimes.com/2006/08/09/technology/09aol.html.

3. Jennifer Preston, "Social Media History Becomes a New Job Hurdle," *New York Times*, July 20, 2011, accessed July 23, 2011, http://www.nytimes.com/2011/07/21/technology/social-media-history-becomes-a-new-job-hurdle.html.

4. Mark Andrejevic has written about these practices as "lateral surveillance: not the top-down monitoring of employees by employers, citizens by the state, but rather the peer-to-peer surveillance of spouses, friends, and relatives." Alice Marwick describes similar dynamics with the term *social surveillance* and observes that our casual everyday engagement with social surveillance helps make all surveillance seem normal. We agree. Mark Andrejevic, "The Work of Watching One Another: Lateral Surveillance, Risk, and Governance," *Surveillance & Society* 2, no. 4 (2005): 479–97, quotation on 481; Alice E. Marwick, "The Public Domain: Social Surveillance in Everyday Life," paper presented at Cyber-Surveillance in Everyday Life: An International Workshop, Toronto, 2011, accessed December 27, 2011, http://www.tiara.org/papers/amarwick_thepublicdomain_2011.pdf.

5. Dan Fletcher, "How Facebook Is Redefining Privacy," *Time*, May 20, 2010, accessed May 22, 2010, http://www.time.com/time/business/article/0,8599,1990582,00.html.

6. "Visualizing Everything Facebook Knows about You."

7. Pete Cashmore, "Privacy Is Dead, and Social Media Hold Smoking Gun," *CNN.com*, October 28, 2009, accessed October 29, 2009, http://edition.cnn.com/2009/OPINION/10/28/cashmore.online.privacy.

8. Fletcher, "How Facebook Is Redefining Privacy."

9. Nicholas Carlson, "Well, These New Zuckerberg IMs Won't Help Facebook's Privacy Problems," *Business Insider*, May 13, 2010, accessed September 28, 2010, http://www.businessinsider.com/well-these-new-zuckerberg-ims-wont-help-facebooks-privacy-problems-2010–5.

10. Kurt Opsahl, "Facebook's Eroding Privacy Policy: A Timeline," *Electronic Frontier Foundation*, April 28, 2010, accessed June 17, 2011, http://www.eff.org/deeplinks/2010/04/facebook-timeline.

11. Ibid.

12. Chris Hoofnagle and Michael Zimmer, "How to Win Friends and Manipulate People," *Huffington Post*, June 2, 2010, accessed July 6, 2010, http://www.huffington post.com/chris-jay-hoofnagle/how-to-win-friends-and-ma_b_598572.html.

13. Jenna Wortham, "Facebook Glitch Brings New Privacy Worries," *New York Times*, May 5, 2010, accessed May 5, 2010, http://www.nytimes.com/2010/05/06/ technology/internet/06facebook.html.

14. Michael Zimmer, "What Happens to Your Facebook Data When You Leave?" *Michael Zimmer.org Blog*, May 10, 2010, accessed July 6, 2010, http://michaelzimmer .org/2010/05/10/what-happens-to-your-facebook-data-when-you-leave.

15. Carolyn Y. Johnson, "Project 'Gaydar,'" *Boston Globe*, September 20, 2009, accessed April 30, 2010, http://www.boston.com/bostonglobe/ideas/articles/ 2009/09/20/project_gaydar_an_mit_experiment_raises_new_questions_about_ online_privacy.

16. Steve Lohr, "Netflix Cancels Contest after Concerns Are Raised about Privacy," *New York Times*, March 12, 2010, accessed March 13, 2010, http://www.nytimes .com/2010/03/13/technology/13netflix.html.

17. Courtney Rubin, "Would You Fire an Employee over a Negative Facebook Post?" *Inc.com*, May 25, 2010, accessed June 17, 2011, http://www.inc.com/news/ articles/2010/05/waitress-fired-for-facebook-post.html.

18. "Canadian Woman Loses Benefits over Facebook Photo," *Seattle Times*, November 21, 2009, accessed June 17, 2011, http://seattletimes.nwsource.com/html/ nationworld/2010327680_apcncanadafacebookinsurance.html.

19. "Break the Law and Your New 'Friend' May Be the FBI," *USA Today*, March 16, 2010, accessed June 17, 2011, http://www.usatoday.com/tech/news/2010–03-16-fbi- facebook_N.htm.

20. Ibid.

21. Ariana Eunjung Cha, "What Sites Such as Facebook and Google Know and Whom They Tell," *Washington Post*, May 29, 2010, accessed June 9, 2010, http://www .washingtonpost.com/wp-dyn/content/article/2010/05/28/AR2010052804853.html.

22. Ibid.

23. Kent German, "Library of Congress to House Your Tweets," *CNet.com*, April 14, 2010, accessed April 26, 2010, http://news.cnet.com/8301–17938_105–20002517-1 .html.

24. https://foursquare.com/about, accessed August 19, 2011; Jenna Wortham, "Telling Friends Where You Are (or Not)," *New York Times*, March 14, 2010, accessed March 15, 2010, http://www.nytimes.com/2010/03/15/technology/15locate .html?adxnnl=1&adxnnlx=1308330756–76Xg2uWUJRP7iJBINnZQow.

25. Ibid.

26. Stephanie Clifford, "Linking Customer Loyalty with Social Networking," *New York Times*, April 28, 2010, accessed April 29, 2010, http://www.nytimes.com/2010/04/ 29/business/media/29adco.html.

27. Stephanie Rosenbloom, "Cellphones Let Shoppers Point, Click and Purchase,"

New York Times, February 26, 2010, accessed February 27, 2010, http://www
.nytimes.com/2010/02/27/business/27shop.html.

28. Stephanie Clifford, "Two-Thirds of Americans Object to Online Tracking," *New York Times*, September 29, 2009, accessed September 30, 2009, http://www.ny times.com/2009/09/30/business/media/30adco.html.

29. Ibid.

30. Claire Cain Miller, "Cellphone in New Role: Loyalty Card," *New York Times*, May 31, 2010, accessed June 1, 2010, http://www.nytimes.com/2010/06/01/ technology/01loopt.html.

31. http://opensource.appleseedproject.org, accessed June 17, 2011.

32. Michael Agger, "Google's Evil Eye: Does the Big G Know Too Much about Us?" *Slate*, October 10, 2007, accessed June 17, 2011, http://www.slate.com/id/2175651.

33. http://www.worldwidewebsize.com, accessed June 17, 2011.

34. Barbaro and Zeller, "Face Is Exposed for AOL Searcher No. 4417749."

35. WiseGeek.com, "How Do Search Engines Work?" *WiseGeek.com* 2010, accessed June 17, 2011, http://www.wisegeek.com/how-do-search-engines-work.htm.

36. Thorsten Joachims, "Learning Retrieval Functions from Implicit Feedback" (2010), accessed June 20, 2010, http://www.cs.cornell.edu/People/tj/career.

37. Barbaro and Zeller, "Face Is Exposed for AOL Searcher No. 4417749."

38. Andrew Turner, "Geolocation by IP Address," *Linux Journal*, October 25, 2004, accessed June 17, 2011, http://www.linuxjournal.com/article/7856. Privacy Rights Clearinghouse, "Fact Sheet 18: Online Privacy: Using the Internet Safely" (2011), accessed June 17, 2011, http://www.privacyrights.org/fs/fs18-cyb.htm. There is a search engine, started in the Netherlands, that doesn't collect IP addresses because of the security concerns mentioned above. It can be found at www.startpage.com, accessed June 17, 2011.

39. Marshall Brain, "How Internet Cookies Work," *HowStuffWorks.com*, April 26, 2000, accessed June 17, 2011, http://computer.howstuffworks.com/cookie3.htm.

40. David Whalen, "The Unofficial Cookie FAQ: Version 2.6," *Cookie Central* 2011, accessed June 17, 2011, http://www.cookiecentral.com/faq. If no expiration date is set on the original text file, it will expire when you close your browser window. Cookies that do not expire during your time online are transferred to your hard drive when you close your browser and are called persistent cookies. They are checked and updated each time a user returns to a website run by the company that originally sent them. They can also be programmed to renew themselves if the user goes back to one of these sites before the initial cookie expires.

41. Jacqui Cheng, "Lawsuit: Disney, Others Spy on Kids with Zombie Cookies," *Ars Technica*, August 16, 2010, accessed June 17, 2011, http://arstechnica.com/tech-policy/news/2010/08/lawsuit-disney-others-spy-on-kids-with-zombie-cookies.ars.

42. Brain, "How Internet Cookies Work."

43. Ryan Singel, "DHS Re-launches Watchlist Help Site after 27B Crushed the Old One," *Threat Level*, February 21, 2007, accessed June 17, 2011, http://www.wired .com/threatlevel/2007/02/dhs_relaunches.

44. Anick Jesdanun, "NSA Inadvertently Uses Banned Data-Tracking 'Cookies' at Website," *USA Today*, December 28, 2005, accessed June 17, 2011, http://www.usatoday.com/tech/news/surveillance/2005-12-28-nsa-cookies_x.htm.

45. Associated Press, "WhiteHouse.gov Uses Cookies, Bugs," *Wired.com*, December 29, 2005, accessed June 17, 2011, http://www.wired.com/techbiz/media/news/2005/12/69945.

46. Eli Pariser, "How the Net Traps Us All in Our Own Little Bubbles," *Guardian*, June 12, 2011, accessed June 15, 2011, http://www.guardian.co.uk/technology/2011/jun/12/google-personalisation-internet-data-filtering?cat=technology&type=article.

47. Ibid.

48. Josh Fox, "Gasland," HBO documentary, 2010, http://www.gaslandthemovie.com.

49. Pariser, "How the Net Traps Us All in Our Own Little Bubbles."

50. Erik Sherman, "Google Grows Non-Ad Revenue Part of Business," *BNet.com*, July 17, 2009, accessed June 17, 2011, http://www.bnet.com/blog/technology-business/google-grows-non-ad-revenue-part-of-business-updated/1222.

51. Stephanie Reese, "Quick Stat: Google to Grab 43.5% Share of US Online Ad Revenues This Year," *eMarketer.com*, May 12, 2011, accessed June 17, 2011, http://www.emarketer.com/blog/index.php/quick-stat-google-grab-435-share-online-ad-revenues-year.

52. Hitwise.com, "Google Share of Searches at 72 Percent for May 2010," *Hitwise.com* 2011, accessed June 17, 2011, http://www.hitwise.com/us/press-center/press-releases/google-searches-may-10.

53. Jeremy Kirk, "Europe Warns Google, Microsoft, Others about Search Data Retention," *Computer World*, May 27, 2010, accessed June 17, 2011, http://www.computerworld.com/s/article/9177424/Europe_warns_Google_Microsoft_others_about_search_data_retention.

54. Rachel Metz, "Google's Growth Makes Privacy Advocates Wary," *MSNBC.com*, November 3, 2008, accessed June 17, 2011, http://www.msnbc.msn.com/id/27517320/ns/technology_and_science-tech_and_gadgets/t/googles-growth-makes-privacy-advocates-wary.

55. Scott Cleland, "What Private Information Google Collects," *GoogleMonitor.com*, May 24, 2010, accessed June 17, 2011, http://googlemonitor.com/wp-content/uploads/2010/05/Google%20Privacy%20Fact%20Sheet.pdf.

56. Paul McDougall, "Exclusive: Gmail Ditched by Major University," *Information Week*, May 5, 2010, accessed December 27, 2011, http://www.informationweek.com/news/windows/224700847.

57. JR Raphael, "Google Voice: 5 Reasons to Use It, 5 Reasons to Think Twice," *PC World*, June 25, 2009, accessed June 17, 2011, http://www.pcworld.com/article/167424-2/google_voice_5_reasons_to_use_it_5_reasons_to_think_twice.html.

58. Craig Walker, Vincent Paquet, and Wesley Chan, "Here Comes Google Voice,"

GoogleBlog.com, March 11, 2009, accessed June 17, 2011, http://googleblog.blogspot
.com/2009/03/here-comes-google-voice.html.

59. Sue Walsh, "Huge Data Breach Hits Google, Hotmail, and Yahoo," *Gadgetell.com*,
   October 6, 2009, accessed June 17, 2011, http://www.gadgetell.com/technologytell/
   article/huge-data-breach-hits-google-hotmail-and-yahoo.

60. Adrian Chen, "GCreep: Google Engineer Stalked Teens, Spied on Chats," *Gawker.
   com* 2010, accessed June 17, 2011, http://m.gawker.com/5637234/gcreep-google-
   engineer-stalked-teens-spied-on-chats?skyline=true&s=i.

61. Ibid.

62. K. C. Jones, "Ex-Computer Consultant Convicted in 'Google Murder' Trial," *Information Week*, November 30, 2005, accessed June 17, 2011, http://www.information
   week.com/news/174403074.

63. Michael Zimmer, "The Externalities of Search 2.0: The Emerging Privacy Threats
   When the Drive for the Perfect Search Engine Meets Web 2.0," *First Monday* 13,
   no. 3 (2008), accessed June 17, 2011, http://www.uic.edu/htbin/cgiwrap/bin/ojs/
   index.php/fm/article/view/2136/1944.

64. Ibid.

65. http://www.torproject.org, accessed June 17, 2011.

66. Bruce Sterling, "From ARPANET to Internet," in *Major Problems in the History
   of American Technology*, ed. Merritt Roe Smith and Gregory Clancey (Boston:
   Houghton Mifflin, 1998).

67. Marguerite Reardon, "The Skinny on Net Neutrality (FAQ)," *CNet.com*, September 13, 2010, accessed June 17, 2011, http://news.cnet.com/8301–30686_3–20015590-
   266.html.

68. Edward Wyatt, "U.S. Court Curbs F.C.C. Authority on Web Traffic," *New York
   Times*, April 6, 2010, accessed June 17, 2011, http://www.nytimes.com/2010/04/07/
   technology/07net.html.

69. David DeGraw, "Shocking Censorship at Google News and the Future of Net Neutrality," *AmpedStatus.com*, April 8, 2010, accessed June 17, 2011, http://ampedstatus
   .com/shocking-censorship-at-google-news-and-the-future-of-net-neutrality.

70. Milton Mueller et al., "DPI and Copyright Protection: A Comparison of EU, US
   and China," paper presented at Cyber-Surveillance in Everyday Life: An International Workshop, May 12–15, 2011, University of Toronto.

71. For instance, in 2009 Joel Tenenbaum, a student at Boston University, was found
   guilty of illegally sharing thirty music files and was ordered to pay the Recording
   Industry Association of America (RIAA) a total of $675,000. In 2010 the courts
   determined that the fine was excessive and reduced it to $67,500. Obviously
   RIAA is intent on making an example of copyright infringers. Ben Sheffner, "Oy
   Tenenbaum! RIAA wins $675,000, or $22,500 per song," *Ars Technica*, July 31,
   2009, accessed June 17, 2011, http://arstechnica.com/tech-policy/news/2009/07/
   o-tenenbaum-riaa-wins-675000-or-22500-per-song.ars. Rosie Swash, "Filesharer
   Joel Tenenbaum Has Fine Reduced by 90%," *Guardian*, July 12, 2010, accessed

June 17, 2011, http://www.guardian.co.uk/music/2010/jul/12/filesharer-joel-tenenbaum.

72. Miguel Helft, "Google Zooms in Too Close for Some," *New York Times*, June 1, 2007, accessed June 17, 2011, http://www.nytimes.com/2007/06/01/technology/01private.html.

73. David Murakami Wood, "Who Killed Bambi?" *Notes from the Ubiquitous Surveillance Society*, January 30, 2009, accessed June 17, 2011, http://ubisurv.wordpress.com/2009/01/30/who-killed-bambi.

74. Kevin J. O'Brien, "Google Data Admission Angers European Officials," *New York Times*, May 15, 2010, accessed June 17, 2011, http://www.nytimes.com/2010/05/16/technology/16google.html.

75. "Google Fined for Street View Privacy Breach," *Huffington Post*, March 21, 2011, accessed July 1, 2011, http://www.huffingtonpost.com/2011/03/21/google-fined-for-street-v_n_838323.html.

76. O'Brien, "Google Data Admission Angers European Officials."

77. Mark Andrejevic, *iSpy: Surveillance and Power in the Interactive Era* (Lawrence: University Press of Kansas, 2007).

78. Kevin Poulsen, "Hacker Disables More than 100 Cars Remotely," *Threat Level*, March 17, 2010, accessed June 17, 2011, http://www.wired.com/threatlevel/2010/03/hacker-bricks-cars.

79. Sean Dodson, "The Net Shapes Up to Get Physical," *Guardian*, October 16, 2008, accessed June 17, 2011, http://www.guardian.co.uk/technology/2008/oct/16/internet-of-things-ipv6.

80. Patrick McGeehan, "Con-Ed Nerve Center Fights to Keep Lights On," *New York Times*, July 7, 2010, accessed June 17, 2011, http://www.nytimes.com/2010/07/08/nyregion/08heat.html.

81. Ken Belson, "Rewarding Those Who Wait to Flip the Switch," *New York Times*, July 21, 2008, accessed June 17, 2011, http://www.nytimes.com/2008/07/21/nyregion/21peak.html.

82. Nick Bilton, "Consumer Watchdog Group Goes after Google," *New York Times*, September 2, 2010, accessed June 17, 2011, http://bits.blogs.nytimes.com/2010/09/02/consumer-watchdog-group-goes-after-google.

83. "Germany to Prevent Facebook Checks," *Newsmax World*, August 25, 2010, accessed June 17, 2011, http://www.newsmaxworld.com/global_talk/eu_germany_facebook_law/2010/08/25/344388.html.

84. "Czechs Halt Google Street View," *BBC News*, September 15, 2010, accessed June 17, 2011, http://www.bbc.co.uk/news/technology-11312390.

Chapter Four

1. Maryclaire Dale, "School Snapped Photos of Students 'Half-Dressed,' in Bed via Webcams, Lawyer Says," *Huffington Post*, April 20, 2010, accessed August 12, 2011, http://www.huffingtonpost.com/2010/04/20/school-webcam-spying-

wors_n_544443.html; Associated Press, "Joshua Levin Sues Lower Merion School District over Emotional Distress for Spying on Laptops," *Huffington Post*, June 8, 2011, accessed August 12, 2011, http://www.huffingtonpost.com/2011/06/08/joshua-levin-lawsuit-merion-spying-laptops_n_873308.html.

2. Jesse J. Holland, "Savana Redding Strip Search Was Illegal, Supreme Court Says," *Huffington Post*, June 25, 2009, accessed August 12, 2011, http://www.huffington post.com/2009/06/25/savana-redding-strip-sear_n_220717.html; Dahlia Lithwick, "Search Me: The Supreme Court Is Neither Hot nor Bothered by Strip Searches," *Slate Magazine*, April 21, 2009, accessed August 12, 2011, http://www.slate.com/id/2216608.

3. "News Report," *Athens (OH) News*, May 28, 1996.

4. John Gilliom, "Lying, Cheating, and Teaching to the Test: The Politics of Surveillance under No Child Left Behind," in *Schools under Surveillance: Cultures of Control in Public Education*, ed. Torin Monahan and Rodolfo D. Torres, 194–212 (New Brunswick, NJ: Rutgers University Press, 2010).

5. Annette Fuentes, *Lockdown High: When the Schoolhouse Becomes a Jailhouse* (London: Verso, 2011); Aaron Kupchik, *Homeroom Security: School Discipline in an Age of Fear* (New York: New York University Press, 2010); Torin Monahan and Rodolfo D. Torres, eds., *Schools under Surveillance: Cultures of Control in Public Education* (New Brunswick, NJ: Rutgers University Press, 2010).

6. Aaron Kupchik and Nicole L. Bracy, "To Protect, Serve, and Mentor? Police Officers in Public Schools," in Monahan and Torres, *Schools under Surveillance*, 21–37; Valerie Steeves, "Online Surveillance in Canadian Schools," in Monahan and Torres, *Schools under Surveillance*, 87–103; Tyler Wall, "'School Ownership Is the Goal': Military Recruiting, Public Schools, and Fronts of War," in Monahan and Torres, *Schools under Surveillance*, 104–20.

7. RaptorWare, "RaptorWare: Visitor Management System," 2011, accessed June 15, 2011, http://www.raptorware.com.

8. Ibid.

9. Garrett Metal Detectors, "News Releases," 2011, accessed August 14, 2011, http://www.creativematters-usa.com/garrett/2-sec-new-releases.html.

10. Ibid.

11. Rachel Dinkes et al., *Indicators of School Crime and Safety: 2007* (Washington, DC: US Department of Education, US Department of Justice, 2007), http://nces.ed.gov//pubs2008/2008021.pdf.

12. Child Welfare Information Gateway, *Child Abuse and Neglect Fatalities: Statistics and Interventions* (Washington, DC: US Department of Health and Human Services, 2008), accessed September 21, 2008, http://www.childwelfare.gov/pubs/factsheets/fatality.cfm#children.

13. Torin Monahan and Rodolfo D. Torres, "Introduction," in Monahan and Torres, *Schools under Surveillance*, 1–18.

14. Torin Monahan, "The Surveillance Curriculum: Risk Management and Social Control in the Neoliberal School," in *Surveillance and Security: Technological Poli-*

tics and Power in Everyday Life, ed. Torin Monahan, 109–24 (New York: Routledge, 2006).

15. Ronnie Casella, "Safety or Social Control? The Security Fortification of Schools in a Capitalist Society," in Monahan and Torres, *Schools under Surveillance*, 73–86.

16. Ibid.; Richard A. Matthew, "Reading, Writing, and Readiness," in Monahan and Torres, *Schools under Surveillance*, 123–39.

17. Rachel Dinkes et al., *Indicators of School Crime and Safety: 2009* (Washington, DC: US Department of Education, US Department of Justice, 2009).

18. Sam Dillon, "Cameras Watching Students, Especially in Biloxi," *New York Times*, September 24, 2003, accessed August 5, 2011, http://www.nytimes.com/2003/09/24/nyregion/cameras-watching-students-especially-in-biloxi.html.

19. Monahan, "Surveillance Curriculum."

20. Paul Hirschfield, "School Surveillance in America: Disparate and Unequal," in Monahan and Torres, *Schools under Surveillance*, 38–54; Monahan and Torres, "Introduction"; Kupchik, *Homeroom Security*.

21. Alan Schwarz, "School Discipline Study Raises Fresh Questions," *New York Times*, July 19, 2011, accessed August 14, 2011, http://www.nytimes.com/2011/07/19/education/19discipline.html.

22. New York Civil Liberties Union, "Zero Tolerance Discipline, Discrimination, and the School to Prison Pipeline" (2011), accessed August 14, 2011, http://www.nyclu.org/files/stpp_fact_sheet.pdf.

23. Catherine Kim, Daniel J. Losen, and Damon Hewitt, *The School to Prison Pipeline: Structuring Legal Reform* (New York: New York University Press, 2010); New York Civil Liberties Union, "Zero Tolerance Discipline."

24. Lauren E. Glaze, *Correctional Populations in the United States, 2009* (US Department of Justice, 2010), accessed August 14, 2011, http://bjs.ojp.usdoj.gov/content/pub/pdf/cpus09.pdf.

25. Michelle Brown, *The Culture of Punishment: Prison Society, and Spectacle* (New York: New York University Press, 2009).

26. Kupchik and Bracy, "To Protect, Serve, and Mentor?"

27. N. L. Bracy, "Circumventing the Law: Students' Rights in Schools with Police," *Journal of Contemporary Criminal Justice* 26, no. 3 (2010): 294–315; Terrence P. Dwyer, "Age and Custody: U.S. Supreme Court Alters the Rules," *PoliceOne.com*, August 5, 2011, accessed August 14, 2011, http://www.policeone.com/juvenile-crime/articles/3907072-Age-and-custody-U-S-Supreme-Court-alters-the-rules.

28. The Supreme Court issued some guidelines in 2011, but blurred boundaries between the activities of SROs and school administrators will most likely continue to complicate the safeguards in practice. Dwyer, "Age and Custody"; Donna St. George, "Supreme Court Ruling, Rising Police Presence in Schools Spur Miranda Questions," *Washington Post*, July 17, 2011, accessed August 14, 2011, http://www.washingtonpost.com/local/education/supreme-court-ruling-rising-police-presence-in-schools-spur-miranda-questions/2011/06/21/gIQAYXgeKI_story.html.

29. Ian Urbina, "It's a Fork, It's a Spoon, It's a . . . Weapon?" *New York Times*, Oc-

tober 11, 2009, accessed August 14, 2011, http://www.nytimes.com/2009/10/12/
education/12discipline.html.

30. Hirschfield, "School Surveillance in America."

31. Susan Saulny, "Twenty-Five Chicago Students Arrested for a Middle-School Food
Fight," *New York Times*, November 10, 2009, accessed August 14, 2011, http://www
.nytimes.com/2009/11/11/us/11foodfight.html.

32. Mitch Johns, "The Honest Truth on Biometrics in Schools," *TMCnet.com*, March
28, 2007, accessed August 3, 2011, http://www.tmcnet.com/biomag/articles/5952-
honest-truth-biometrics-schools.htm.

33. For example, myschoolacount.com or cashlessschools.com, accessed August 3,
2011.

34. Marie Lingblom, "School Cafeteria's Biometrics System Gets Good Grades," *CRN.
com*, March 28, 2003, accessed August 3, 2011, http://www.crn.com/18822229/
printablearticle.htm.

35. Some commentators argue that fingerprinting will reduce stigma for students
receiving federally subsidized meals because they won't be treated differently from
other students. This might be true in some school settings, but many schools now
have separate cafeteria lines for the purchase of à la carte items such as a Pizza
Hut pizza or Taco Bell burritos. Because federal guidelines rule out unhealthful
food of this sort but most students prefer it, kids receiving subsidized meals often
choose not to eat rather than mark themselves as poor. This stigma would not be
solved by fingerprint systems because poor students would still have to choose the
"uncool" line. Jeremy Nobile, "Middle School to Get Finger Scanners," *Tallmadge
Express.com*, November 28, 2010, accessed August 3, 2011, http://www.tallmadge
express.com/news/article/4938443; Bettina Elias Siegel, "A la Carte—a World
Apart?" *TheLunchTray.com*, July 15, 2010, accessed August 3, 2011, http://www
.thelunchtray.com/a-la-carte-a-world-apart; Carol Pogash, "Free Lunch Isn't Cool,
So Some Students Go Hungry," *New York Times*, March 1, 2008, accessed August 3,
2011, http://www.nytimes.com/2008/03/01/education/01lunch.html?_r=1&scp=
7&sq=too%20cool%20lunch&st=cse.

36. Johns, "Honest Truth on Biometrics in Schools."

37. Margaret K. Nelson, *Parenting Out of Control: Anxious Parents in Uncertain Times*
(New York: New York University Press, 2010).

38. Lingblom, "School Cafeteria's Biometrics System Gets Good Grades."

39. Debra Lau Whelan, "MA District Nixes Biometrics Plan While Technology
Spreads in Schools Nationwide," *School Library Journal*, May 1, 2007, accessed
August 3, 2011, http://www.libraryjournal.com/slj/printissuecurrentissue/863143–
427/finger_scanning_in_schools_raises.html.csp.

40. "Scottish School Uses Palm Reading Biometrics in Cafeteria," *Homeland Security
Newswire*, October 30, 2006, accessed August 3, 2011, http://www.homeland
securitynewswire.com/scottish-school-uses-palm-reading-biometrics-cafeteria.

41. American Civil Liberties Union, "ACLU of Massachusetts Praises Decision to
Cancel Lunch Bytes Program," April 19, 2007, accessed August 3, 2011, http://www

.aclu.org/technology-and-liberty/aclu-massachusetts-praises-decision-cancel-lunch-bytes-program; Whelan, "MA District Nixes Biometrics Plan."

42. Heather Sells, "Would You Let Them Scan Your Child?" *CBN News*, January 12, 2006, accessed August 3, 2011, http://catholicforum.fisheaters.com/index .php?topic=1510972.0;wap2.

43. Ibid.

44. Los Angeles Almanac, "Largest Public and Private High Schools in Los Angeles County, 2008–2009" (2009), accessed August 4, 2011, http://www.laalmanac.com/education/ed15.htm.

45. Torin Monahan, *Globalization, Technological Change, and Public Education* (New York: Routledge, 2005).

46. Ibid.

47. Jennifer Radcliffe, "Tracking Devices Used in School Badges," *Houston Chronicle*, October 11, 2010, accessed August 4, 2011, http://www.chron.com/disp/story.mpl/metropolitan/7241100.html.

48. Ibid.

49. Kim Zetter, "School RFID Plan Gets an F," *Wired.com*, February 10, 2005, accessed August 4, 2011, http://www.wired.com/politics/security/news/2005/02/66554.

50. James Heiser, "Schools Track Students with RFID Chips," *New American*, October 13, 2010, accessed August 4, 2011, http://thenewamerican.com/culture/education/4867-schools-track-students-with-rfid-chips.

51. Radcliffe, "Tracking Devices Used in School Badges."

52. Zetter, "School RFID Plan Gets an F."

53. Radcliffe, "Tracking Devices Used in School Badges."

54. Ibid.

55. Nicole Ozer, "Don't Let Schools Chip Your Kids" (American Civil Liberties Union, 2010), accessed August 4, 2011, http://www.aclu.org/blog/technology-and-liberty/dont-let-schools-chip-your-kids.

56. Jonathan Chevreau, "Can Hackers Read RFID Chips on Credit Cards?" *National Post*, March 16, 2010, accessed August 4, 2011, http://network.nationalpost.com/NP/blogs/wealthyboomer/archive/2010/03/16/can-hackers-read-rfid-chips-on-credit-cards.aspx.

57. Josh Fischman, "Blackboard Gets into Video Surveillance," *Chronicle of Higher Education*, March 10, 2008, accessed August 14, 2011, http://chronicle.com/blogs/wiredcampus/blackboard-gets-into-video-surveillance/3747.

58. FreelanceVenue.com, "[JOB OFFER] Get Paid to Write Test Questions," 2010, accessed August 14, 2011, http://www.freelancevenue.com/26/job-offer-get-paid-to-write-test-questions.html. See also Thomas Toch, *Margins of Error: The Education Testing Industry in the No Child Left Behind Era* (Washington, DC: Education Sector, 2006).

59. Gilliom, "Lying, Cheating, and Teaching to the Test"; M. Gail Jones, Brett D. Jones, and Tracy Hargrove, *The Unintended Consequences of High-Stakes Testing* (New York: Rowman and Littlefield, 2003).

60. Alfie Kohn, "Fighting the Tests: A Practical Guide to Rescuing Our Schools," *Phi Delta Kappan* 82, no. 5 (2001): 348–57.

61. Jeneba Ghatt, "Atlanta's Cheating Ways: School Officials Changed Test Scores," *Washington Times*, July 7, 2011, accessed August 14, 2011, http://communities washingtontimes.com/neighborhood/politics-raising-children/2011/jul/7/atlantas-cheating-ways-school-officials-test-score.

62. Jack Gillum and Marisol Bello, "When Standardized Test Scores Soared in D.C., Were the Gains Real?" *USA Today*, March 30, 2011, accessed August 14, 2011, http://www.usatoday.com/news/education/2011-03-28-1Aschooltesting28_CV_N .htm.

63. Ibid.

64. Jen Weiss, "Scan This: Examining Student Resistance to School Surveillance," in Monahan and Torres, *Schools under Surveillance*, 213–29.

65. Fernanda Santos, "Protest over Metal Detectors Gains Legs as Students Walk Out," *New York Times*, September 21, 2005, accessed August 14, 2011, http://www .nytimes.com/2005/09/21/nyregion/21walkout.html?ex=1284955200&en=9ada77d 5bd9a239f&ei=5090&partner=rssuserland&emc=rss.

66. Weiss, "Scan This."

67. Ibid.

68. Ibid.; Kupchik, *Homeroom Security*.

69. Andrew Hope, "Seductions of Risk, Social Control, and Resistance to School Surveillance," in Monahan and Torres, *Schools under Surveillance*, 230–46.

70. Michel Foucault, *Discipline and Punish: The Birth of the Prison* (New York: Vintage, 1977).

Chapter Five

1. Mark Andrejevic, *iSpy: Surveillance and Power in the Interactive Era* (Lawrence: University Press of Kansas, 2007), 65.

2. Frederick Winslow Taylor, *The Principles of Scientific Management* (New York: Harper and Brothers, 1911).

3. Frederick W. Taylor, "The Principles of Scientific Management" (1911), in *Major Problems in the History of American Technology*, ed. Merritt Roe Smith and Gregory Clancey (Boston: Houghton Mifflin, 1998), 274.

4. See also Alfred DuPont Chandler, *The Visible Hand: The Managerial Revolution in American Business* (Cambridge, MA: Belknap Press, 1977).

5. Maurice W. Bowen, "Arsenal Workers Strike" (1913), in Smith and Clancey, *Major Problems in the History of American Technology*, 282–83.

6. Merritt Roe Smith and Gregory Clancey, "Inventing Efficiency: Scientific Management, ca 1900–1940," in Smith and Clancey, *Major Problems in the History of American Technology*, 267–68.

7. James J. Flink, "Modern Times," in Smith and Clancey, *Major Problems in the History of American Technology*, 349.

8. Ibid.

9. Andrejevic, *iSpy*, 71–72.

10. Arnold's, "Tractor Guidance Systems—GPS Systems—Autoguidance Systems" (2011), accessed July 21, 2011, http://www.arnoldsinc.com/specials_guidance.htm.

11. Christian Parenti, *The Soft Cage: Surveillance in America, from Slavery to the War on Terror* (New York: Basic Books, 2003); Kirstie Ball, "Workplace Surveillance: An Overview," *Labor History* 51, no. 1 (2010): 87–106.

12. http://www.guardian.co.uk/uk/2010/nov/11/surveillance-society-soon-reality.

13. Parenti, *Soft Cage*, 131.

14. Andrew Wineke and Wayne Heilman, "Colorado Springs: Call Center Nation," *Colorado Springs Gazette*, May 9, 2010, accessed July 21, 2011, http://www.gazette.com/articles/call-98346-thomas-handle.html.

15. Disgusted, "TSG Hell," *Cable Rant*, August 7, 2007, accessed July 21, 2011, http://www.cablerant.com/index.php?topic=27.0.

16. Keith Dawson, *The Call Center Handbook: The Complete Guide to Starting, Running and Improving Your Call Center*, 5th ed. (San Francisco, CA: CMP Books, 2004), 62.

17. Ball, "Workplace Surveillance."

18. Parenti, *Soft Cage*, 137–38.

19. Urban Dictionary, "E-Slave," 2011, accessed July 21, 2011, http://www.urban dictionary.com/define.php?term=E-Slave.

20. Kirstie Ball, "Categorizing the Workers: Electronic Surveillance and Social Ordering in the Call Center," in *Surveillance as Social Sorting: Privacy, Risk, and Digital Discrimination*, ed. David Lyon (New York: Routledge, 2003), 202.

21. Wineke and Heilman, "Colorado Springs: Call Center Nation."

22. Although people tend to think of call centers as being in India or other countries overseas, the latest move is to bring them back to the United States, especially to workers' homes. Companies believe this "phonesourcing" or "homesourcing" can increase customer satisfaction and still save money because they don't have to pay for office space. Of course, except for the visual surveillance, this doesn't mean employee monitoring dissipates. It probably does mean workers are more insecure: paid when needed and fired with ease. Carolyn Beeler, "Outsourced Call Centers Return, to U.S. Homes," *National Public Radio*, August 25, 2010, accessed July 23, 2011, http://www.npr.org/templates/story/story.php?storyId=129406588&ps=cprs; "Indian Call Centers: Coming to America?" *Week*, August 20, 2010, accessed October 13, 2010, http://theweek.com/article/index/206212/indian-call-centers-coming-to-america.

23. Parenti, *Soft Cage*, 138.

24. Current Employee, "Go Daddy—'For a Call Center It's Probably Better than Average,'" *GlassDoor.com*, June 4, 2010, accessed July 23, 2011, http://www.glassdoor.com/Reviews/Employee-Review-Go-Daddy-RVW520248.htm.

25. Kirstie Ball et al., "Democracy, Surveillance and 'Knowing What's Good for You':

The Private Sector Origins of Profiling and the Birth of 'Citizen Relationship Management,'" in *Surveillance and Democracy*, ed. Kevin D. Haggerty and Minas Samatas (New York: Routledge, 2010).

26. Institute for Management Excellence, "February 2008—Dealing with 'Problem' Employees" (2008), accessed October 16, 2010, http://www.itstime.com/feb2008 .htm.

27. Richard E. Sclove, *Democracy and Technology* (New York: Guilford Press, 1995).

28. Ibid.

29. Billing potential includes all the diagnostic tests patients are given. Hospitals also make money in many other ways, such as elective surgeries and expensive end-of-life care.

30. Torin Monahan and Jill A. Fisher, "Surveillance Impediments: Recognizing Obduracy with the Deployment of Hospital Information Systems," *Surveillance & Society* 9, no. 1/2 (2011): 1–16.

31. Ibid.

32. Ibid.

33. Jill A. Fisher and Torin Monahan, "Tracking the Social Dimensions of RFID Systems in Hospitals," *International Journal of Medical Informatics* 77, no. 3 (2008): 176–83.

34. Monahan and Fisher, "Surveillance Impediments."

35. Ibid.; Jill A. Fisher, "Indoor Positioning and Digital Management: Emerging Surveillance Regimes in Hospitals," in *Surveillance and Security: Technological Politics and Power in Everyday Life*, ed. Torin Monahan, 77–88 (New York: Routledge, 2006).

36. Fisher, "Indoor Positioning and Digital Management."

37. Sprint Enterprises, "Testimonials" (2010), accessed October 12, 2010, http://www .sprintbarcontrols.com/Testimonials.page.

38. David C. Wyld, "Radio Frequency Identification: Advanced Intelligence for Table Games in Casinos," *Cornell Hospitality Quarterly* 49, no. 2 (2008): 134–44.

39. Mark Gruetze, "Casino Surveillance Theme: 'I'll Be Watching You,'" *Pittsburgh Tribune Review*, April 29, 2011, accessed July 24, 2011, http://www.pittsburghlive .com/x/pittsburghtrib/ae/gambling/s_734644.html#.

40. Carlos Serrao, "The New Deal," *Wired Magazine*, February 1, 2004, accessed July 24, 2011, http://www.wired.com/wired/archive/12.02/start_pr.html.

41. Gruetze, "Casino Surveillance Theme."

42. Wyld, "Radio Frequency Identification."

43. Serrao, "New Deal."

44. Surveillance Source, "Casino Surveillance: Theft Prevention" (2011), accessed July 24, 2011, http://www.surveillance-source.com/Casino_Surveillance.htm.

45. Terry Austrin and Jackie West, "Skills and Surveillance in Casino Gaming: Work, Consumption and Regulation," *Work, Employment and Society* 19, no. 2 (2005): 305–26.

46. Ibid.

47. Lorraine Bayard de Volo, "Service and Surveillance: Infrapolitics at Work among Casino Cocktail Waitresses," *Social Politics* 10, no. 3 (2003): 347–76.

48. David J. Lender, "Treppel v. Biovail Corp.," *eDiscoverings*, June 2008, accessed October 13, 2010, http://www.weil.com/news/pubdetail.aspx?pub=7825; Michael Orey, "Corporate Snoops," *Businessweek*, October 9, 2006, accessed October 13, 2010, http://www.businessweek.com/magazine/content/06_41/b4004008.htm.

49. Dealbook, "Biovail C.E.O. Sues Former Analyst for Slander," *Dealbook*, June 26, 2007, accessed October 13, 2010, http://dealbook.nytimes.com/2007/06/26/biovail-ceo-sues-former-analyst-for-slander/#more-15313.

50. Stephen Shankland, "HP Chairman: Use of Pretexting 'Embarrassing,'" *CNet News*, September 8, 2006, accessed October 13, 2010, http://news.cnet.com/HP-chairman-use-of-pretexting-embarrassing/2100–1014_3–6113715.html; "Ousted HP Chairwoman to Surrender," *CBS News*, February 11, 2009, accessed October 13, 2010, http://www.cbsnews.com/stories/2006/10/05/business/main2068862.shtml.

51. "Ousted HP Chairwoman to Surrender."

52. Leslie Katz, "Calif. Court Drops Charges against Dunn," *CNet News*, March 14, 2007, accessed October 13, 2010, http://news.cnet.com/Calif.-court-drops-charges-against-Dunn/2100–1014_3–6167187.html.

53. Orey, "Corporate Snoops."

54. Ibid.

55. Amy Goodman, "Eamon Javers on the Secret World of Corporate Espionage and Moonlighting CIA Operatives," *Democracy Now!* February 9, 2010, accessed October 13, 2010, http://www.democracynow.org/2010/2/9/eamon_javers_on_the_secret_world.

56. Orey, "Corporate Snoops."

57. "Corporate Espionage: Are You Being Watched?" *Forbes.com*, September 15, 2006, accessed October 13, 2010, http://www.pallorium.com/ARTICLES/art43.html.

58. Brad Knickerbocker, "Rupert Murdoch Phone-Hacking Scandal: US Connections Grow," *Christian Science Monitor*, July 16, 2011, accessed July 23, 2011, http://www.csmonitor.com/USA/2011/0716/Rupert-Murdoch-phone-hacking-scandal-US-connections-grow. As with most scandals, the writing was on the wall much earlier: Kim Zetter, "Murdoch Reporters' Phone-Hacking Was Endemic, Victimized Hundreds," *Threat Level*, September 2, 2010, accessed July 23, 2011, http://www.wired.com/threatlevel/2010/09/murdoch-phone-hacking; "Pair Jailed over Royal Phone Taps," *BBC News*, January 26, 2007, accessed July 24, 2011, http://news.bbc.co.uk/2/hi/uk_news/6301243.stm.

59. John Gilliom, *Surveillance, Privacy, and the Law: Employee Drug Testing and the Politics of Social Control* (Ann Arbor: University of Michigan Press, 1994).

60. At almost every step of the way there have been court challenges to the legality of widespread drug-testing programs. Courts have found them to be an intense invasion of privacy, an unnecessary degradation, a hopelessly inaccurate method, and

a fundamental violation of constitutional rights. Other courts, however (including the ever important Supreme Court), have found urine tests to be a minimal and acceptable intrusion that is an important part of fighting the War on Drugs.

61. Jennifer Preston, "Social Media History Becomes a New Job Hurdle," *New York Times*, July 20, 2011, accessed July 23, 2011, http://www.nytimes.com/2011/07/21/technology/social-media-history-becomes-a-new-job-hurdle.html.

62. Ibid. At the moment, applicants must consent to these formal background checks, but if agreeing is required to be considered for a job, who would opt out?

63. Jackie Cohen, "ALERT: Job Screening Agency Archiving All Facebook," *All Facebook: The Unofficial Facebook Resource*, June 20, 2011, accessed July 23, 2011, http://www.allfacebook.com/alert-job-screening-agency-archiving-all-facebook-2011–06.

64. Preston, "Social Media History Becomes a New Job Hurdle"; Mathew Ingram, "Yes, Virginia, HR Execs Check Your Facebook Page," *Gigaom.com*, January 27, 2010, accessed July 23, 2011, http://gigaom.com/2010/01/27/yes-virginia-hr-execs-check-your-facebook-page.

65. Preston, "Social Media History Becomes a New Job Hurdle."

66. Ibid.

67. Ibid.

68. Social Intelligence, "Social Media Monitoring" (2011), accessed July 23, 2011, http://www.socialintelligencehr.com/monitoring.

69. Taylor, *Principles of Scientific Management*, accessed July 23, 2011, http://ecuip.lib.uchicago.edu/diglib/social/chi1919/dline/d2/taylor_f.html.

70. Gilliom, *Surveillance, Privacy, and the Law*, 74.

71. Ball, "Workplace Surveillance."

72. Ibid.; Loril M. Gossett and Julian Kilker, "My Job Sucks: Examining Counter-institutional Web Sites as Locations for Organizational Member Voice, Dissent, and Resistance," *Management Communication Quarterly* 20, no. 1 (2006): 63–90.

Chapter Six

1. Wayne Drash, "Doctors Question TSA's Use of Pat Downs, Body Scans," *CNN.com*, November 23, 2010, accessed November 25, 2010, http://www.cnn.com/2010/HEALTH/11/23/holiday.travel.medical/index.html.

2. Jake Tapper et al., "White House: Terrorists Have Discussed Use of Prosthetics to Conceal Explosives," *ABC News*, November 22, 2010, accessed November 25, 2010, http://abcnews.go.com/Travel/tsa-responds-passenger-outrages-underwear-search-happen/story?id=12208932.

3. Samantha Murphy, "Mad as Hell: Airport Security Screening Protests Mount," *MSNBC.com*, November 16, 2010, accessed November 25, 2010, http://www.msnbc.msn.com/id/40222780; ibid.

4. Marci Stone, "John Tyner Refuses TSA Airport X-Ray Security Screening and Faces Fine" (video), *Examiner.com*, November 15, 2010, accessed June 7, 2011,

http://www.examiner.com/us-headlines-in-national/john-tyner-refuses-tsa-airport-x-ray-security-screening-and-faces-fine-video.

5. Associated Press, "Planned Airport Protests Fail to Take Off," *MSNBC.com* 2010, accessed November 25, 2010, http://www.msnbc.msn.com/id/40351426/ns/travel.

6. Ibid.

7. CBC News, "Quebec Man Changes Name to Dodge Relentless Airport Screening," *CBC News*, September 11, 2008, accessed May 25, 2011, http://www.cbc.ca/news/canada/montreal/story/2008/09/11/nofly-name.html.

8. Johanna Neuman, "Terrorist Watch List at Airports Tops 1 Million Names," *Los Angeles Times*, July 15, 2008, accessed May 25, 2011, http://latimesblogs.latimes.com/presidentbush/2008/07/terrorist-watch.html.

9. Alan Travis, "US to Store Passenger Data for 15 Years," *Guardian*, May 25, 2011, accessed May 26, 2011, http://www.guardian.co.uk/world/2011/may/25/us-to-store-passenger-data?cat=world&type=article.

10. Alexander Chee, "Face Recognition Software Thinks Asians Are Blinking," *Koreanish.com*, August 20, 2009, accessed May 26, 2011, http://koreanish.com/2009/08/20/face-recognition-software-thinks-asians-are-blinking; Shoshana Magnet, *When Biometrics Fail: Gender, Race, and the Technology of Identity* (Durham, NC: Duke University Press, 2011).

11. Magnet, *When Biometrics Fail.*

12. Shoshana Magnet, "Are Biometrics Race-Neutral?" *blog*on*nymity: Blogging on the Identity Trail*, June 5, 2007, accessed May 26, 2011, http://www.anonequity.org/weblog/archives/2007/06/are_biometrics_raceneutral.php.

13. American Civil Liberties Union, "Stop Racial Profiling at American Airports!" *ACLU.org*, October 6, 2002, accessed May 27, 2011, http://www.aclu.org/stop-racial-profiling-american-airports.

14. Jane McLean, "What Is a NEXUS Card," *About.com* (2011), accessed May 27, 2011, http://gocanada.about.com/od/canadatravelplanner/qt/nexus_card.htm.

15. Cheryl Sullivan, "US Cancels 'Virtual Fence' along Mexican Border: What's Plan B?" *Christian Science Monitor*, January 15, 2011, accessed May 27, 2011, http://www.csmonitor.com/USA/2011/0115/US-cancels-virtual-fence-along-Mexican-border.-What-s-Plan-B. "Napolitano Cancels Virtual Border Fence Project, Proposes Alternative," *FoxNews.com*, January 14, 2011, accessed May 27, 2011, http://www.foxnews.com/politics/2011/01/14/napolitano-cancels-virtual-border-fence-project-proposes-alternative.

16. Sullivan, "US Cancels 'Virtual Fence.'"

17. Torin Monahan, *Surveillance in the Time of Insecurity* (New Brunswick, NJ: Rutgers University Press, 2010).

18. Sullivan, "US Cancels 'Virtual Fence'"; National Guard Bureau, "National Guard Members Will Assist DHS/CBP/ICE by Engaging in Counter-Narcotic Missions on the Southwest Border," *The National Guard—Southwest Border Mission* 2011, accessed May 30, 2011, http://www.ng.mil/features/Border/default.aspx.

19. www.blueservo.net, accessed May 30, 2011.

20. Hille Koskela, "'Did You Spot an Alien?' Voluntary Vigilance, Borderwork and the Texas Virtual Border Watch Program," *Space and Polity* 14, no. 2 (2010): 103–21; Hille Koskela, "'Don't Mess with Texas!' Texas Virtual Border Watch Program and the (Botched) Politics of Responsibilization," *Crime, Media, Culture* 7, no. 1 (2011): 49–66; Texas Border Sheriff's Coalition, "The Texas Border Sheriff's Coalition Institute Border Surveillance Cameras," November 20, 2008, accessed May 28, 2011, http://www.epcounty.com/CS/blogs/sheriff_news/archive/2008/11/20/texas-border-sheriff-s-coalition-institute-border-surveillance-cameras.aspx.

21. Amy Goodman, "Vigilantes or Civilian Border Patrol? A Debate on the Minuteman Project," *DemocracyNow.org*, April 5, 2005, accessed May 28, 2011, http://www.democracynow.org/2005/4/5/vigilantes_or_civilian_border_patrol_a; James P. Walsh, "From Border Control to Border Care: The Political and Ethical Potential of Surveillance," *Surveillance & Society* 8, no. 2 (2010): 113–30.

22. American Civil Liberties Union, "ACLU of Arizona Denounces Unlawful Imprisonment of Immigrant by Minuteman Volunteer," *ACLU.org*, April 7, 2005, accessed May 28, 2011, http://www.aclu.org/immigrants-rights/aclu-arizona-denounces-unlawful-imprisonment-immigrant-minuteman-volunteer.

23. Wayne A. Cornelius, "Death at the Border: Efficacy and Unintended Consequences of US Immigration Control Policy," *Population and Development Review* 27, no. 4 (2001): 661–85; Torin Monahan, "Questioning Surveillance and Security," in *Surveillance and Security: Technological Politics and Power in Everyday Life*, ed. Torin Monahan, 1–23 (New York: Routledge, 2006); Nicole Santa Cruz, "Border Deaths in Arizona May Break Record," *Los Angeles Times*, August 24, 2010, accessed May 28, 2011, http://articles.latimes.com/2010/aug/24/nation/la-na-border-deaths-20100824.

24. Walsh, "From Border Control to Border Care," 118.

25. Ibid.

26. Irma van der Ploeg, "The Illegal Body: 'Eurodac' and the Politics of Biometric Identification," *Ethics and Information Technology* 1 (1999): 295–302.

27. Ibid., 297.

28. Miriam Ticktin, "Where Ethics and Politics Meet: The Violence of Humanitarianism in France," *American Ethnologist* 33, no. 1 (2006): 33–49.

29. Miriam Ticktin, "Policing and Humanitarianism in France: Immigration and the Turn to Law as State of Exception," *Interventions* 7, no. 3 (2005): 347–68; Ticktin, "Where Ethics and Politics Meet."

30. Van der Ploeg, "Illegal Body," 299.

31. European Commission, "EU to Use EURODAC Fingerprint Database to Fight Serious Crime and Terrorism," *TheGovMonitor.com*, September 10, 2009, accessed May 28, 2011, http://www.thegovmonitor.com/world_news/europe/eu-to-use-eurodac-fingerprint-database-to-fight-serious-crime-and-terrorism-4413.html.

32. This section draws on Tyler Wall and Torin Monahan, "Surveillance and Violence from Afar: The Politics of Drones and Liminal Security-Scapes," *Theoretical Criminology* 15, no. 3 (2011): 239–54; for further detail, see the full article. See

also Scott Lindlaw, "Remote-Control Warriors Suffer Battle Stress at a Distance: Psychologists, Chaplains Ease Mental Strain," *Boston.com*, August 8, 2008, accessed June 7, 2011, http://www.boston.com/news/nation/articles/2008/08/08/remote_control_warriors_suffer_battle_stress_at_a_distance.

33. Christopher Drew, "Drones Are Weapons of Choice in Fighting Qaeda," *New York Times*, March 16, 2009, accessed June 7, 2011, http://www.nytimes.com/2009/03/17/business/17uav.html?_r=1&hp.

34. United States Air Force, "'Reaper' Moniker Given to MQ-9 Unmanned Aerial Vehicle," *US Air Force*, September 14, 2006, accessed June 7, 2011, http://www.af.mil/news/story.asp?storyID=123027012&page=2.

35. Ibid.

36. Peter Bergen and Katherine Tiedemann, "The Year of the Drone," *New America Foundation*, February 24, 2010, accessed June 7, 2011, http://counterterrorism.newamerica.net/sites/newamerica.net/files/policydocs/bergentiedemann2.pdf.

37. Noah Shachtman, "Drone School, a Ground's-Eye View," *Wired Magazine*, May 27, 2005, accessed June 7, 2011, http://www.wired.com/science/discoveries/news/2005/05/67655?currentPage=all.

38. Lindlaw, "Remote-Control Warriors Suffer Battle Stress at a Distance."

39. Afshin Rattansi, "'Knowing When to Say When': Meet Lt. Col. Chris Gough; Killing by Drone and Proud of It," *Counterpunch*, April 2–4, 2010, accessed June 7, 2011, http://www.counterpunch.org/rattansi04022010.html.

40. Lindlaw, "Remote-Control Warriors Suffer Battle Stress at a Distance."

41. Siobhan Gorman, Yochi J. Dreazen, and August Cole, "Insurgents Hack U.S. Drones," *Wall Street Journal*, December 17, 2009, accessed June 26, 2010, http://online.wsj.com/article/SB126102247889095011.html.

42. Dave Gilson, "Predators vs. Aliens: Arizona Wants More Drones," *Mother Jones*, May 26, 2010, accessed June 7, 2011, http://motherjones.com/mojo/2010/05/predator-drones-UAV-border-arizona; Canwest News Service, "U.S. Readying Drones to Monitor Canadian Border," *Canada.com*, January 9, 2007, accessed June 7, 2011, http://www.canada.com/topics/news/story.html?id=ecf2d42c-0b78–40c5–8011–648dab3d0620&p=1.

43. Sullivan, "US Cancels 'Virtual Fence.'"

44. Declan McCullagh and Anne Broache, "FBI Taps Cell Phone Mic as Eavesdropping Tool," *CNET News*, December 1, 2006, accessed June 7, 2011, http://news.cnet.com/FBI-taps-cell-phone-mic-as-eavesdropping-tool/2100–1029_3–6140191.html.

45. Wall and Monahan, "Surveillance and Violence from Afar."

46. "Pilotless Police Drone Takes Off," *BBC News*, May 21, 2007, accessed May 29, 2011, http://news.bbc.co.uk/2/hi/uk_news/england/merseyside/6676809.stm.

47. Monahan, "Questioning Surveillance and Security"; Jeffrey Rosen, "Being Watched—a Cautionary Tale for a New Age of Surveillance," *New York Times Magazine*, October 7, 2001, accessed June 7, 2011, http://www.nytimes.com/2001/10/07/magazine/07SURVEILLANCE.html.

48. David Murakami Wood, Kirstie Ball, David Lyon, Clive Norris, and Charles Raab, "A Report on the Surveillance Society" (Wilmslow, UK: Office of the Information Commissioner, 2006). See also Michael McCahill and Clive Norris, "Estimating the Extent, Sophistication and Legality of CCTV in London," in M. Gill, ed. *CCTV*, 51–66 (Leicester: Perpetuity Press, 2003).

49. David Murakami Wood, "The Total Surveillance Society?" *Notes from the Ubiquitous Surveillance Society*, January 25, 2011, accessed June 7, 2011, http://ubisurv .wordpress.com/2011/01/25/the-total-surveillance-society.

50. Naomi Klein, "China Unveils Frightening Futuristic Police State at Olympics," *Huffington Post*, August 8, 2008, accessed August 20, 2008, http://www.alternet .org/story/94278.

51. Jia Feishang, "Spy Camera Numbers to Double," *ShanghaiDaily.com*, May 27, 2011, accessed May 29, 2011, http://www.shanghaidaily.com/nsp/Metro/2011/05/27/Spy %2Bcamera%2Bnumbers%2Bto%2Bdouble.

52. Klein, "China Unveils Frightening Futuristic Police State at Olympics."

53. Ibid.

54. Ibid.

55. Ibid.

56. Colin J. Bennett and Kevin D. Haggerty, *Security Games: Surveillance and Control at Mega-Events* (New York: Routledge, 2011).

57. Minas Samatas, "Surveilling the 2004 Athens Olympics in the Aftermath of 9/11: International Pressures and Domestic Implications" (n.d.), accessed May 31, 2011, http://www.soc.uoc.gr/social/prosopiko/samatas/Samatas_SURVEILLING_ ATHENS_2004%20.pdf; Nicole Itano, "As Olympic Glow Fades, Athens Questions $15 Billion Cost," *Christian Science Monitor*, July 21, 2008, accessed May 31, 2011, http://www.csmonitor.com/World/2008/0721/p04s01-wogn.html.

58. Greece, for instance, has since faced a devastating financial crisis that has threatened Europe's overall economy and led to severe, unpopular cutbacks in social services.

59. Thomas K. Grose, "London Admits It Can't Top Lavish Beijing Olympics When It Hosts 2012 Games," *USNews.com*, August 22, 2008, accessed May 31, 2011, http:// www.usnews.com/news/world/articles/2008/08/22/london-admits-it-cant-top- lavish-beijing-olympics-when-it-hosts-2012-games; Foreign Policy, "The List: Five Ways Beijing Will Be the Biggest, Baddest Olympics Ever," *ForeignPolicy .com*, July 26, 2008, accessed May 31, 2011, http://www.foreignpolicy.com/articles/ 2008/07/25/the_list_five_ways_beijing_will_be_the_biggest_baddest_olympics _ever.

60. Jennifer King, Deirdre Mulligan, and Steven Raphael, *CITRIS Report: The San Franciscos Community Safety Camera Program* (Berkeley, CA: Center for Information Technology Research in the Interest of Society, 2008), accessed June 5, 2011, www.muniwireless.com/reports/sf-video-study-2008.pdf; Marcus Nieto, *Public Video Surveillance: Is It an Effective Crime Prevention Tool?* (Sacramento: California Research Bureau, 1997), http://www.library.ca.gov/CRB/97/05.

61. David Murakami Wood, "Chicago: The Future of US CCTV?" *Notes from the Ubiquitous Surveillance Society*, February 21, 2009, accessed June 7, 2011, http://ubisurv.wordpress.com/2009/02/21/chicago-the-future-of-us-cctv.

62. Adrian Hearn, "New Camera Can Catch Motorists Committing Five Different Offences," *Small World News Service*, November 2, 2010, accessed June 28, 2011, http://swns.com/new-camera-can-catch-motorists-committing-five-different-offences-021014.html.

63. Cynthia Freschi, "A Smart Future for Video Surveillance," *SecurityMagazine.com*, January 1, 2009, accessed June 1, 2011, http://www.securitymagazine.com/articles/a-smart-future-for-video-surveillance-1.

64. Murakami Wood, "Chicago: The Future of US CCTV?"; IBM Press Room, "The City of Chicago's OEMC and IBM Launch Advanced Video Surveillance System," *IBM*, September 27, 2007, accessed June 1, 2011, http://www-03.ibm.com/press/us/en/pressrelease/22385.wss.

65. David Murakami Wood, "The City Where the Cameras Never Sleep . . . New York, New York," *Notes from the Ubiquitous Surveillance Society*, September 21, 2010, accessed June 7, 2011, http://ubisurv.wordpress.com/2010/09/21/the-city-where-the-cameras-never-sleep-new-york-new-york.

66. Marco Frezzella, "Weltneuheit: Videotechnologie lässt Objekte verschwinden," October 9, 2010, accessed June 1, 2011, http://www.tu-ilmenau.de/journalisten/pressemeldungen/einzelnachricht/newsbeitrag/5784; David Murakami Wood, "Real-Time Video Erasure?" *Notes from the Ubiquitous Surveillance Society*, October 14, 2010, accessed June 7, 2011, http://ubisurv.wordpress.com/2010/10/14/real-time-video-erasure.

67. Murakami Wood, "Real-Time Video Erasure?"

68. Mark Klein, "Wiretap Whistle-Blower's Account," *Wired Magazine*, April 7, 2006, accessed June 2, 2011, http://www.wired.com/science/discoveries/news/2006/04/70621.

69. Ibid.

70. Torin Monahan, "Surveillance and Terrorism," in *Routledge Handbook of Surveillance Studies*, eds. Kirstie Ball, Kevin D. Haggerty, and David Lyon, 285–91 (London: Routledge, 2012).

71. Ibid.

72. James Risen and Eric Lichtblau, "Bush Lets U.S. Spy on Callers without Courts," *New York Times*, December 16, 2005, accessed June 7, 2011, http://www.nytimes.com/2005/12/16/politics/16program.html.

73. Robert O'Harrow Jr., "Centers Tap into Personal Databases; State Groups Were Formed after 9/11," *Washington Post*, April 2, 2008.

74. Michael German and Jay Stanley, "What's Wrong with Fusion Centers?" December 2007, http://www.aclu.org/files/pdfs/privacy/fusioncenter_20071212.pdf; Monahan, *Surveillance in the Time of Insecurity*.

75. Jeremy Scahill, "Blackwater's Private Spies," *Nation (Online)*, June 5, 2008, accessed August 20, 2008, http://www.thenation.com/doc/20080623/scahill.

76. WikiLeaks, "Collateral Murder: Transcript" (2010), accessed June 4, 2011, http://www.collateralmurder.com/en/transcript.html.

77. Ibid.

78. Steve Breyman, "Wikileaks Strikes Again. Afghanistan: The Inside Story," July 27, 2010, accessed June 4, 2011, http://www.counterpunch.com/breyman07272010.html.

79. Declan Walsh, "WikiLeaks Cables Portray Saudi Arabia as a Cash Machine for Terrorists," *Guardian*, December 5, 2010, accessed June 4, 2011, http://www.guardian.co.uk/world/2010/dec/05/wikileaks-cables-saudi-terrorist-funding.

80. Brandon Keim, "WikiLeaks Reveals International Intrigue over Science and Environment," *Wired Magazine*, January 12, 2011, accessed June 4, 2011, http://www.wired.com/wiredscience/2011/01/wikileaks-and-science.

81. After facing a backlash that threatened to shut it down, in 2011 WikiLeaks released its full collection of diplomatic cables in unredacted form. Although this move was heavily criticized as having the potential to endanger people acting as sources in other countries, a subsequent independent investigation by the Associated Press found that few if any sources were endangered. Nancy A. Youssef, "Officials May Be Overstating the Danger from WikiLeaks," *McClatchy Newspapers*, November 28, 2010, accessed June 4, 2011, http://www.mcclatchydc.com/2010/11/28/104404/officials-may-be-overstating-the.html; Bradley Klapper and Cassandra Vinograd, "AP Review Finds No Threatened WikiLeaks Sources," *Seattle Times*, September 10, 2011, accessed December 27, 2011, http://seattletimes.nwsource.com/html/nationworld/2016163616_apuswikileaks.html; Raphael G. Satter, "WikiLeaks Reveals All, Media Groups Criticize Move," *Chicago Sun-Times*, September 2, 2011, accessed December 27, 2011, http://www.suntimes.com/news/world/7422995–418/wikileaks-reveals-all-media-groups-criticize-move.html.

82. David Murakami Wood, "The Internet Must Be Defended!" *Notes from the Ubiquitous Surveillance Society*, December 7, 2010, accessed June 4, 2011, http://ubisurv.wordpress.com/2010/12/07/the-internet-must-de-defended; Ellen Nakashima and Jerry Markon, "WikiLeaks Founder Could Be Charged under Espionage Act," *Washington Post*, November 30, 2010, accessed June 4, 2011, http://www.washingtonpost.com/wp-dyn/content/article/2010/11/29/AR2010112905973.html. Note also that Julian Assange was accused of sexual assault in 2010 and that Sweden sought his extradition from England for those charges.

83. Glenn Greenwald, "The Inhumane Conditions of Bradley Manning's Detention," *Salon*, December 15, 2010, accessed June 4, 2011, http://www.salon.com/news/opinion/glenn_greenwald/2010/12/14/manning.

84. Murakami Wood, "Internet Must Be Defended!"

85. David Murakami Wood, "The Internet Must Be Defended (2): A Transparency (R)evolution?" *Notes from the Ubiquitous Surveillance Society*, December 10, 2010, accessed June 4, 2011, http://ubisurv.wordpress.com/2010/12/10/open-source-revolution; Mark Andrejevic, *iSpy: Surveillance and Power in the Interactive Era* (Lawrence: University Press of Kansas, 2007).

86. Monahan, "Questioning Surveillance and Security."
87. Monahan, "Surveillance and Terrorism."
88. Ibid.

Conclusion

1. We use the term *citizen* in a broad and inclusive way that is not restricted to your legal relation to the state. *Citizen*, in our sense, refers to a person in the world, subject to governance but possessing autonomy, will, and rights.
2. Christena E. Nippert-Eng, *Islands of Privacy* (Chicago: University of Chicago Press, 2010).
3. Kevin D. Haggerty and Richard V. Ericson, "The Surveillant Assemblage," *British Journal of Sociology* 51, no. 4 (2000): 605–22.
4. For a particularly good read on this, see Murray Edelman, *Constructing the Political Spectacle* (Chicago: University of Chicago Press, 1988).
5. James C. Scott, *Weapons of the Weak: Everyday Forms of Peasant Resistance* (New Haven, CT: Yale University Press, 1985).

FURTHER EXPLORATIONS

Here you'll find a collection of books and a few online resources that can help you continue your exploration of surveillance. This is not an exhaustive bibliography but a selective collection of readings we think might be interesting and accessible to our readers. To control the size of the list, we've chosen to omit articles published in magazines and scholarly journals. Sources are in alphabetical order within general categories of interest.

Organizations Dedicated to Research, Education, and Advocacy on Surveillance Issues

American Civil Liberties Union: www.aclu.org
Big Brother Watch (UK): www.bigbrotherwatch.org.uk
Electronic Frontier Foundation: www.eff.org
Electronic Privacy Information Center: www.epic.org
Privacy International: www.privacyinternational.org
Privacy Rights Clearinghouse: www.privacyrights.org
Statewatch: www.statewatch.org
Surveillance Studies Center: www.sscqueens.org
Surveillance Studies Network: www.surveillance-studies.net

Other Online Resources

Notes from the Ubiquitous Surveillance Society blog: ubisurv.wordpress.com
Surveillance and Identity blog: surveillantidentity.blogspot.com
Surveillance & Society (journal): www.surveillance-and-society.org
Surveillance Studies listserv: www.jiscmail.ac.uk/archives/surveillance.html
Surveillance Studies blog (mostly in German): www.surveillance-studies.org

Overviews of Academic Research on Surveillance

Ball, Kirstie, Kevin D. Haggerty, and David Lyon, eds. 2012. *Routledge Handbook of Surveillance Studies*. New York: Routledge.

Hier, Sean P., and Josh Greenberg, eds. 2007. *The Surveillance Studies Reader*. New York: McGraw-Hill.

Lyon, David. 2007. *Surveillance Studies: An Overview*. Cambridge: Polity Press.

Biometrics

Gates, Kelly. 2011. *Our Biometric Future: Facial Recognition Technology and the Culture of Surveillance*. New York: New York University Press.

Magnet, Shoshana. 2011. *When Biometrics Fail: Gender, Race, and the Technology of Identity*. Durham, NC: Duke University Press.

Mueller, Benjamin J. 2010. *Security, Risk and the Biometric State: Governing Borders and Bodies*. New York: Routledge.

van der Ploeg, Irma. 2005. *The Machine-Readable Body: Essays on Biometrics and the Informatization of the Body*. Maastricht, Netherlands: Shaker.

Consumption, Interactivity, and Social Media

Andrejevic, Mark. 2007. *iSpy: Surveillance and Power in the Interactive Era*. Lawrence: University Press of Kansas.

Fuchs, Christian, Kees Boersma, Anders Albrechtslund, and Marisol Sandoval, eds. 2011. *Internet and Surveillance: The Challenges of Web 2.0 and Social Media*. New York: Routledge.

Mayer-Schönberger, Viktor. 2009. *Delete: The Virtue of Forgetting in the Digital Age*. Princeton, NJ: Princeton University Press.

O'Harrow, Robert. 2005. *No Place to Hide*. New York: Free Press.

Slack, Jennifer Daryl, and J. Macgregor Wise. 2005. *Culture and Technology: A Primer*. New York: Peter Lang.

Turow, Joseph. 2006. *Niche Envy: Marketing Discrimination in the Digital Age*. Cambridge, MA: MIT Press.

Culture, Art, and Media

Levin, Thomas Y., Ursula Frohne, and Peter Weibel, eds. 2002. *CTRL [Space]: Rhetorics of Surveillance from Bentham to Big Brother*. Cambridge, MA: MIT Press.

McGrath, John E. 2004. *Loving Big Brother: Performance, Privacy and Surveillance Space*. New York: Routledge.

Shepard, Mark, ed. 2011. *Sentient City: Ubiquitous Computing, Architecture, and the Future of Urban Space*. Cambridge, MA: MIT Press.

Surveillance Camera Players. 2006. *We Know You Are Watching*. New York: Factory School.

Geographies of Surveillance

Adey, Peter. 2010. *Aerial Life: Spaces, Mobilities, Affects*. Malden, MA: Wiley-Blackwell.

Andrzejewski, Anna Vemer. 2008. *Building Power: Architecture and Surveillance in Victorian America*. Knoxville: University of Tennessee Press.

Coaffee, Jon, David Murakami Wood, and Peter Rogers. 2009. *The Everyday Resilience of the City: How Cities Respond to Terrorism and Disaster*. Basingstoke, UK: Palgrave Macmillan.

Graham, Stephen. 2010. *Cities under Siege: The New Military Urbanism*. London: Verso.

Graham, Stephen, and Simon Marvin. 2001. *Splintering Urbanism: Networked Infrastructures, Technological Mobilities and the Urban Condition*. New York: Routledge.

Kitchin, Rob, and Martin Dodge. 2011. *Code/Space: Software and Everyday life*. Cambridge, MA: MIT Press.

Monmonier, Mark S. 2002. *Spying with Maps: Surveillance Technologies and the Future of Privacy*. Chicago: University of Chicago Press.

Shepard, Mark, ed. 2011. *Sentient City: Ubiquitous Computing, Architecture, and the Future of Urban Space*. Cambridge, MA: MIT Press.

Sorkin, Michael, ed. 2007. *Indefensible Space: The Architecture of the National Insecurity State*. New York: Routledge.

Globalizing Surveillance

Bennett, Colin J., and Charles D. Raab. 2006. *The Governance of Privacy: Policy Instruments in Global Perspective*. 2nd ed. Cambridge, MA: MIT Press.

Murakami Wood, David. 2012. *The Watched World: Globalization and Surveillance*. Lanham, MD: Rowman and Littlefield.

Rule, James B., and G. W. Greenleaf, eds. 2008. *Global Privacy Protection: The First Generation*. Northampton, MA: Elgar.

Samatas, Minas. 2004. *Surveillance in Greece: From Anticommunist to Consumer Surveillance*. New York: Pella.

Zureik, Elia, David Lyon, and Yasmeen Abu-Laban, eds. 2011. *Surveillance and Control in Israel/Palestine: Population, Territory and Power*. New York: Routledge.

Zureik, Elia, L. Lynda Harling Stalker, Emily Smith, David Lyon, and Yolande E. Chan, eds. 2010. *Surveillance, Privacy, and the Globalization of Personal Information: International Comparisons*. Montreal: McGill-Queen's University Press.

Identification and Identity

Barnard-Wills, David. 2012. *Surveillance and Identity: Discourse, Subjectivity and the State*. Burlington, VT: Ashgate.

Bennett, Colin J., and David Lyon, eds. 2008. *Playing the Identity Card: Surveillance, Security and Identification in Global Perspective*. New York: Routledge.

Cole, Simon A. 2001. *Suspect Identities: A History of Fingerprinting and Criminal Identification.* Cambridge, MA: Harvard University Press.

Kerr, Ian, Valerie Steeves, and Carole Lucock, eds. 2009. *Lessons from the Identity Trail: Anonymity, Privacy, and Identity in a Networked Society.* Oxford: Oxford University Press.

Lyon, David. 2009. *Identifying Citizens: ID Cards as Surveillance.* Cambridge: Polity.

Magnet, Shoshana. 2011. *When Biometrics Fail: Gender, Race, and the Technology of Identity.* Durham, NC: Duke University Press.

Robertson, Craig. 2010. *The Passport in America: The History of a Document.* New York: Oxford University Press.

Torpey, John C. 2000. *The Invention of the Passport: Surveillance, Citizenship, and the State.* Cambridge: Cambridge University Press.

Policing and Crime

Brown, Michelle. 2009. *The Culture of Punishment: Prison, Society, and Spectacle.* New York: New York University Press.

Coleman, Roy, and Michael McCahill. 2011. *Surveillance and Crime.* Thousand Oaks, CA: Sage.

Deflem, Mathieu, ed. 2008. *Surveillance and Governance: Crime Control and Beyond.* Bingley, UK: Emerald.

Ericson, Richard V., and Kevin D. Haggerty. 1997. *Policing the Risk Society.* Toronto: University of Toronto Press.

Garland, David. 2001. *The Culture of Control: Crime and Social Order in Contemporary Society.* Chicago: University of Chicago Press.

Haggerty, Kevin D. 2001. *Making Crime Count.* Toronto: University of Toronto Press.

Huey, Laura. 2007. *Negotiating Demands: The Politics of Skid Row Policing in Edinburgh, San Francisco, and Vancouver.* Toronto: University of Toronto Press.

Marks, Amber. 2008. *Headspace: Sniffer Dogs, Spy Bees and One Woman's Adventures in the Surveillance Society.* London: Virgin Books.

Marx, Gary T. 1988. *Undercover: Police Surveillance in America.* Berkeley: University of California Press.

Norris, Clive, and Dean Wilson, eds. 2006. *Surveillance, Crime, and Social Control.* Burlington, VT: Ashgate.

Simon, Jonathan. 2007. *Governing through Crime: How the War on Crime Transformed American Democracy and Created a Culture of Fear.* Oxford: Oxford University Press.

Wacquant, Loïc J. D. 2009. *Punishing the Poor: The Neoliberal Government of Social Insecurity.* Durham, NC: Duke University Press.

Popular Books

Doctorow, Cory. 2008. *Little Brother.* New York: Tom Doherty Associates.

Laidler, Keith. 2008. *Surveillance Unlimited: How We've Become the Most Watched People on Earth.* Cambridge, UK: Icon Books.

O'Harrow, Robert. 2005. *No Place to Hide*. New York: Free Press.

Parenti, Christian. 2003. *The Soft Cage: Surveillance in America, from Slavery to the War on Terror*. New York: Basic Books.

Webb, Maureen. 2007. *Illusions of Security: Global Surveillance and Democracy in the Post-9/11 World*. San Francisco, CA: City Lights Books.

Privacy

Agre, Philip E., and Marc Rotenberg, eds. 1997. *Technology and Privacy: The New Landscape*. Cambridge, MA: MIT Press.

Bennett, Colin J. 2008. *The Privacy Advocates: Resisting the Spread of Surveillance*. Cambridge, MA: MIT Press.

Cohen, Julie E. 2012. *Configuring the Networked Self: Law, Code, and the Play of Everyday Practice*. New Haven, CT: Yale University Press.

Goold, Benjamin J., and Daniel Neyland, eds. 2009. *New Directions in Surveillance and Privacy*. Portland, OR: Willan.

Nippert-Eng, Christena E. 2010. *Islands of Privacy*. Chicago: University of Chicago Press.

Nissenbaum, Helen Fay. 2010. *Privacy in Context: Technology, Policy, and the Integrity of Social Life*. Stanford, CA: Stanford Law Books.

Nock, Steven L. 1993. *The Costs of Privacy: Surveillance and Reputation in America*. New York: Aldine de Gruyter.

Regan, Priscilla M. 1995. *Legislating Privacy: Technology, Social Values, and Public Policy*. Chapel Hill: University of North Carolina Press.

Rosen, Jeffrey. 2001. *The Unwanted Gaze: The Destruction of Privacy in America*. New York: Vintage Books.

Rule, James B. 1973. *Private Lives and Public Surveillance: Social Control in the Computer Age*. London: Allen Lane.

———. 2007. *Privacy in Peril: How We Are Sacrificing a Fundamental Right in Exchange for Security and Convenience*. Oxford: Oxford University Press.

Slobogin, Christopher. 2007. *Privacy at Risk: The New Government Surveillance and the Fourth Amendment*. Chicago: University of Chicago Press.

Solove, Daniel J. 2004. *The Digital Person: Technology and Privacy in the Information Age*. New York: New York University Press.

———. 2008. *Understanding Privacy*. Cambridge, MA: Harvard University Press.

Race, Class, Gender, and Surveillance

Eubanks, Virginia. 2011. *Digital Dead End: Fighting for Social Justice in the Information Age*. Cambridge, MA: MIT Press.

Gandy, Oscar H. 1993. *The Panoptic Sort: A Political Economy of Personal Information*. Boulder, CO: Westview.

———. 2009. *Coming to Terms with Chance: Engaging Rational Discrimination and Cumulative Disadvantage*. Burlington, VT: Ashgate.

Gilliom, John. 2001. *Overseers of the Poor: Surveillance, Resistance, and the Limits of Privacy*. Chicago: University of Chicago Press.

Lyon, David, ed. 2003. *Surveillance as Social Sorting: Privacy, Risk, and Digital Discrimination*. New York: Routledge.

Magnet, Shoshana. 2011. *When Biometrics Fail: Gender, Race, and the Technology of Identity*. Durham, NC: Duke University Press.

Mirzoeff, Nicholas. 2011. *The Right to Look: A Counterhistory of Visuality*. Durham, NC: Duke University Press.

Monahan, Torin, ed. 2006. *Surveillance and Security: Technological Politics and Power in Everyday Life*. New York: Routledge.

———. 2010. *Surveillance in the Time of Insecurity*. New Brunswick, NJ: Rutgers University Press.

Schools

Casella, Ronnie. 2006. *Selling Us the Fortress: The Promotion of Techno-security Equipment for Schools*. New York: Routledge.

Devine, John. 1996. *Maximum Security: The Culture of Violence in Inner-City Schools*. Chicago: University of Chicago Press.

Kupchik, Aaron. 2010. *Homeroom Security: School Discipline in an Age of Fear*. New York: New York University Press.

Lyons, William, and Julie Drew. 2006. *Punishing Schools: Fear and Citizenship in American Public Education*. Ann Arbor: University of Michigan Press.

Monahan, Torin. 2005. *Globalization, Technological Change, and Public Education*. New York: Routledge.

Monahan, Torin, and Rodolfo D. Torres, eds. 2010. *Schools under Surveillance: Cultures of Control in Public Education*. New Brunswick, NJ: Rutgers University Press.

Security

Altheide, David L. 2009. *Terror Post 9/11 and the Media*. New York: Peter Lang.

Ball, Kirstie, and Frank Webster, eds. 2003. *The Intensification of Surveillance: Crime, Terrorism and Warfare in the Information Age*. Sterling, VA: Pluto Press.

Bennett, Colin J., and Kevin D. Haggerty, eds. 2011. *Security Games: Surveillance and Control at Mega-events*. New York: Routledge.

Bigo, Didier, and Anastassia Tsoukala, eds. 2008. *Terror, Insecurity and Liberty: Illiberal Practices of Liberal Regimes after 9/11*. New York: Routledge.

Fussey, Peter, Jon Coaffee, Gary Armstrong, and Dick Hobbs. 2011. *Securing and Sustaining the Olympic City: Reconfiguring London for 2012 and Beyond*. Burlington, VT: Ashgate.

Lyon, David. 2003. *Surveillance after September 11*. Malden, MA: Polity Press.

Monahan, Torin, ed. 2006. *Surveillance and Security: Technological Politics and Power in Everyday Life*. New York: Routledge.

———. 2010. *Surveillance in the Time of Insecurity*. New Brunswick, NJ: Rutgers University Press.

Mueller, Benjamin J. 2010. *Security, Risk and the Biometric State: Governing Borders and Bodies*. New York: Routledge.

Rosen, Jeffrey. 2004. *The Naked Crowd: Reclaiming Security and Freedom in an Anxious Age*. New York: Random House.

Salter, Mark B., ed. 2008. *Politics at the Airport*. Minneapolis: University of Minnesota Press.

Solove, Daniel J. 2011. *Nothing to Hide: The False Tradeoff between Privacy and Security*. New Haven, CT: Yale University Press.

Surveillance in Everyday Life

Aas, Katja Franko, Helene Oppen Gundhus, and Heidi Mork Lomell, eds. 2009. *Technologies of InSecurity: The Surveillance of Everyday Life*. New York: Routledge-Cavendish.

Lyon, David. 1994. *The Electronic Eye: The Rise of Surveillance Society*. Minneapolis: University of Minnesota Press.

———. 2001. *Surveillance Society: Monitoring Everyday Life*. Philadelphia, PA: Open University.

Monahan, Torin, ed. 2006. *Surveillance and Security: Technological Politics and Power in Everyday Life*. New York: Routledge.

Nelson, Margaret K. 2010. *Parenting Out of Control: Anxious Parents in Uncertain Times*. New York: New York University Press.

Nelson, Margaret K., and Anita Ilta Garey, eds. 2009. *Who's Watching? Daily Practices of Surveillance among Contemporary Families*. Nashville, TN: Vanderbilt University Press.

Staples, William G. 2000. *Everyday Surveillance: Vigilance and Visibility in Postmodern Life*. Lanham, MD: Rowman and Littlefield.

Theorizing Surveillance

Bogard, William. 1996. *The Simulation of Surveillance: Hypercontrol in Telematic Societies*. Cambridge: Cambridge University Press.

Dandeker, Christopher. 1990. *Surveillance, Power, and Modernity: Bureaucracy and Discipline from 1700 to the Present Day*. Cambridge: Polity Press.

Foucault, Michel. 1977. *Discipline and Punish: The Birth of the Prison*. New York: Vintage.

Giddens, Anthony. 1990. *The Consequences of Modernity*. Stanford, CA: Stanford University Press.

Haggerty, Kevin D., and Richard V. Ericson, eds. 2006. *The New Politics of Surveillance and Visibility*. Toronto: University of Toronto Press.

Haggerty, Kevin D., and Minas Samatas, eds. 2010. *Surveillance and Democracy*. New York: Routledge.

Poster, Mark. 1990. *The Mode of Information: Poststructuralism and Social Context*. Chicago: University of Chicago Press.

Rose, Nikolas S. 1999. *Powers of Freedom: Reframing Political Thought*. New York: Cambridge University Press.

Scott, James C. 1998. *Seeing Like a State: How Certain Schemes to Improve the Human Condition Have Failed*. New Haven, CT: Yale University Press.

Video Surveillance

Doyle, Aaron, Randy K. Lippert, and David Lyon, eds. 2012. *Eyes Everywhere: The Global Growth of Camera Surveillance*. New York: Routledge.

Goold, Benjamin J. 2004. *CCTV and Policing: Public Area Surveillance and Police Practices in Britain*. Oxford: Oxford University Press.

Hier, Sean P. 2010. *Panoptic Dreams: Streetscape Video Surveillance in Canada*. Vancouver: UBC Press.

McCahill, Michael. 2002. *The Surveillance Web: The Rise of Visual Surveillance in an English City*. Cullompton, UK: Willan.

Neyland, Daniel. 2006. *Privacy, Surveillance and Public Trust*. New York: Palgrave Macmillan.

Norris, Clive, and Gary Armstrong. 1999. *The Maximum Surveillance Society: The Rise of CCTV*. Oxford: Berg.

Smith, Gavin. 2012. *Opening the Black Box: The Everyday Life of Surveillance*. New York: Routledge.

Workplaces

Gilliom, John. 1994. *Surveillance, Privacy, and the Law: Employee Drug Testing and the Politics of Social Control*. Ann Arbor: University of Michigan Press.

Lyon, David. 2007. *Surveillance Studies: An Overview*. Cambridge: Polity Press.

Parenti, Christian. 2003. *The Soft Cage: Surveillance in America, from Slavery to the War on Terror*. New York: Basic Books.

Staples, William G. 2000. *Everyday Surveillance: Vigilance and Visibility in Postmodern Life*. Lanham, MD: Rowman and Littlefield.

INDEX